CARICATURES AND THE CONSTITUTION 1760 -1832

Series Editor: Michael Duffy

The other titles in this series are:

The Common People and Politics 1750–1790s *by John Brewer*
The Englishman and the Foreigner *by Michael Duffy*
Walpole and the Robinocracy *by Paul Langford*
Religion in the Popular Prints 1600–1832 *by John Miller*
Crime and the Law in English Satirical Prints 1600–1832 *by J.A. Sharpe*
The American Revolution *by Peter D.G. Thomas*

THE ENGLISH SATIRICAL PRINT 1600 -1832

Caricatures and the Constitution 1760 - 1832

by H T Dickinson

CHADWYCK-HEALEY

CAMBRIDGE

First published 1986

ISBN 0-85964-171-6

Chadwyck-Healey Ltd
Cambridge Place, Cambridge CB2 1NR England

Chadwyck-Healey Inc.
1021 Prince Street, Alexandria, VA 22314 USA

British Library Cataloguing in Publication Data

Dickinson, H. T.
 Caricatures and the Constitution, 1760–1832.—
 (The English satirical print, 1600–1832)
 1. Prints, English.   2. Satire, English—History
 and criticism   3. Constitutions in art   4. Great
 Britain in art
 I. Title   II. Series
 769′.493441022   NE962.C6

Library of Congress Cataloging in Publication Data

Dickinson, H. T.
 Caricatures and the Constitution, 1760–1832.

 (The English satirical print, 1600–1832)
 Bibliography: p.
 1. Great Britain—Constitutional history—Caricatures
 and cartoons.   2. Great Britain—Politics and government
 —1760–1830—Caricatures and cartoons.   3. English wit
 and humor, Pictorial.   I. Title.   II. Series.
 DA195.D45   1985   941.07   85-5957

Printed by Unwin Brothers Limited, Old Woking, Surrey

CONTENTS

Publisher's Note   7
General Editor's Preface   9
Introduction   11
   The Political Role of Caricatures   11
   The Prints and the Constitution   23
   Footnotes   41
The Plates   43
Further Reading   345

PUBLISHER'S NOTE

In 1978 Chadwyck-Healey published *English Cartoons and Satirical Prints 1320-1832 in the British Museum* in which the 17,000 prints listed in the *Catalogue of Political and Personal Satires* by F. G. Stephens and M. D. George are reproduced on microfilm identified by their catalogue numbers.

British Museum Publications reprinted the Stephens and George catalogue to accompany the microfilm edition and for the first time it became possible for scholars to study the prints that are so exhaustively described in Stephens and George, without needing to visit the Department of Prints and Drawings.

It also made this series possible for it is doubtful whether the seven authors would ever have been able to spend the time in the British Museum necessary to search through this huge collection. As it was they each had access to the microfilm edition which they used for their research.

The reprint of the Stephens and George catalogue is itself now out of print but has been reissued on microfilm by Chadwyck-Healey.

GENERAL EDITOR'S PREFACE

In the course of the seventeenth and eighteenth centuries the English satirical print emerged as a potent vehicle for the expression of political and social opinion. Their development was slow at first, but picking up pace from the 1720s, the prints stood out by the 1780s as the most striking symbol of the freedom of the press in England. Sold usually individually, as works of art as well as of polemic, by the late eighteenth century they constituted the basis of a thriving commercial industry and had established themselves as one of the predominant art forms of the age. The graphic skill of the engraver as well as the pungency of his message makes the English satirical print an immensely attractive, entertaining and very fruitful source for the study of Stuart and Hanoverian England. Surprisingly, although many of the prints survive, this source has been frequently neglected, and it is the aim of this series to remedy that deficiency by showing through the study of selected aspects of the period between 1600 and 1832 how the historian can illuminate the prints and prints can illuminate history. All art forms are the product of particular political and social environments, and this volume together with the rest of the series hopes to set this particular art form – the English satirical print – in its proper historical context by revealing how it gave graphic representation to the ideas, assumptions and environment of that era.

Michael Duffy

INTRODUCTION

I.
The Political Role of Caricatures

A 'closed society', in which political power is limited to a narrow segment of the population, needs to keep a firm control over both the dissemination and the expression of political opinions. The press, in particular, has to be subjected to strict censorship and its output restricted to those with a vested interest in defending the existing political and social systems. In contrast, the hallmarks of an 'open society' are the easy exchange of information and the free interplay of opinion, especially by means of an active press. The press flourishes best in a political society that is committed more to the task of persuasion than to government repression and opposition subversion. How far the growth of the press is the cause, and how far the effect, of a more open society it is difficult, perhaps impossible, to answer. What cannot be disputed is that, in Britain, the progress of the press towards the role of a 'fourth estate' of the realm, something that was achieved between the 1760s and the 1830s, was intimately concerned with the campaign to reform the political institutions of the nation. During these decades the press matured and established itself to the point where its impact upon political developments was significant, while the campaign for parliamentary reform eventually became irresistible.

Much has been written about the attempts to reform the constitution between 1760 and the passing of the Reform Bill in 1832. Much has also been written about the growth of the press during the same period. Numerous efforts have been made to connect the two developments. Not enough, however, has been done to connect the campaign for parliamentary reform with the huge increase in political caricatures and graphic satires during these years. Political caricature was only a part of the larger journalism which included newspapers, periodicals, pamphlets and books, but it was a rapidly growing and distinctive media outlet for political expression and it deserves closer study. Political caricature was particularly well suited to be both a reflector and a shaper of public opinion. Its relatively simple and succinct messages and its brightly-coloured pictures could be understood by large sections of the population from the highly educated to the barely literate. Although it engaged in uninhibited criticism the graphic satire was more difficult to suppress than the pamphlet or the newspaper. It was in fact accorded greater freedom from government interference and legal harassment. On the other hand, it has to be admitted that graphic satire could cope with some ideas far more effectively than with others. In seeking to understand more fully the relationship between political caricature and the constitution we need to appreciate the issues involved in the defence of the constitution and the campaign for constitutional changes and also the extent to which these issues found their way into the political prints.

1. THE CIRCULATION OF POLITICAL PRINTS

In examining the long debates about the merits and defects of the constitution between 1760 and 1832 too much emphasis should not be laid upon either government repression or the threat of revolution. Civil liberties were occasionally infringed by government action, but an authoritarian regime was never established. While a small minority of radicals did plot revolution, the overwhelming majority of reformers rejected the use of force as the means of achieving parliamentary reform. Rational argument and moral persuasion were the chief weapons of both those who wished to defend and those who wished to reform the constitution. The conservatives exploited the press and set up loyalist organisations. The reformers campaigned by means of petitions and platform speeches, by associating peacefully in clubs, societies and massed marches. Both sides hoped to achieve success by converting public opinion to their cause and they reached more people by means of the printing press than by any other method. Those who were determined to defend the existing constitution engaged in a war of words and a conflict of ideas just as much as the reformers. Governments might restrict the civil liberties of the people, might hire spies to penetrate radical organisations, might intimidate reformers with treason trials and the occasional display of naked force, but at no stage did they erect a police state in which the expression of political dissent was impossible. The conservative defenders of the existing constitution were well aware that they too could succeed only so long as they carried a significant body of opinion along with them. To this end they engaged in a propaganda campaign to confirm the public in their support for the old constitution. In the end, however, they lost the argument. The Reform Bill of 1832 was passed when opinion within parliament as well as opinion 'out-of-doors' no longer had confidence in the old constitution.

The arguments for and against parliamentary reform were developed most fully in newspapers, periodicals and pamphlets, but they can also be followed in the political caricatures of the late eighteenth and early nineteenth centuries. The production of political prints, like the sales of the press in general, owed much to political developments. Production tended to grow over the period from 1760 to 1832 although the rise was not continuous. Some years showed a marked increase in output, while in nearly all years more political prints appeared in late autumn and early spring, when parliament was in session, than in the other months of the year. In the 1760s political prints appeared at the rate of about one per week at most. By the 1770s this rate of production had risen by about fifty per cent. From the 1780s to the early 1800s political prints appeared at the rate of about four per week on average. For the 1810s and 1820s the average rate of production was some twenty per cent higher than this. In the crisis years of 1830 to 1832 the rate of production varied between seven and ten political prints per week. Throughout this period there were other indications of the growing significance of political prints. In the 1760s and 1770s the production of political prints was lower than that of social prints. After 1788 the number of political prints produced each year was nearly always higher than the number of social prints. The disparity was particularly marked in the crisis years of 1813 to 1816, 1819 to 1821, and 1829 to 1832. Spectacular production rates for political prints were always reached in years of political tension. An average of three to five political prints appeared each week in the years 1803, 1809, 1815, 1819, 1821 and 1829. An average of six to ten political prints appeared each week in 1770, 1784, 1820, 1830, 1831 and 1832. In these years the political prints not only benefited from the high level of public interest in politics, but from the fact that they could capitalise on the dramatic involvement of particular individuals. In 1770 it was Wilkes and Liberty, in 1784 it was the intense rivalry between Pitt and Fox, in 1820 it was the trial of Queen Caroline, and in 1830 to 1832 it was the confrontation between Wellington and Grey, which provided superb material for the caricaturists. Further evidence that the political print was gradually becoming a recognised and accepted method of criticism can be elicited from the rise in the number of prints that were signed by their creators. In the early 1760s nearly all the prints were anonymous and the exceptions were mainly the social satires. By the 1780s more than half the political prints were signed and by the 1820s almost all political prints were signed. It is also significant that there were sharp decreases in the number of signed prints when political tension was particularly high and unrest was widespread; that is, in 1817 to 1820 and 1831 to 1832.[1]

The general rise in the production of political prints in the late eighteenth and early nineteenth centuries and the quite spectacular production rates in certain years provide clear evidence of the connection between political tension and the appearance of political prints. Some historians have argued that the political prints reached a mass audience and could reach the illiterate sectors of the population more effectively than any other product of the public press. These claims are easily made, but rather difficult to verify. The available evidence suggests that most prints had rather a limited circulation among the political elite and the propertied middle classes of London and Westminster, but that some prints reached a much wider audience. It is impossible to be certain of the press runs of any of the political prints. Some of the prints by amateur artists may have had runs as low as one or two hundred. The majority of political prints probably sold about five hundred copies. Copperplate engravings were slow to produce and the plate deteriorated after a few hundred pressings. The most popular prints by the most successful professional artists may have produced between 1,000 and 1,500 copies from a single plate. A new plate would be produced only if the print was a very considerable success. In most years therefore the total production of political prints is unlikely to have exceeded 50,000 and only in exceptional years would the annual production rate have been as high as 200,000 political prints. Such figures are far lower than the total annual sales for newspapers which was over 7 million in 1750, over 16 million in 1801 and over 30 million in the early 1830s. On the other hand, a few political prints did have exceptional sales. Hogarth's famous portrait of Wilkes (*Plate 6*)* as a cunning and impudent demagogue, sold about 4,000 copies within a few weeks in 1763.[2] Benjamin Wilson's *The Repeal, or the Funeral of Miss Ame-Stamp* (*9*) was reputed to have sold 2,000 copies in four days. Several pirated editions soon appeared and it has been estimated that as many as 16,000 copies were sold in 1766.[3] Far more successful than such prints which sold as individual caricatures were those which appeared as illustrations in popular publications. In the late 1760s and early 1770s several newspapers and periodicals, including John Almon's *Political Register*, the *Public Advertiser*, the *London Magazine*, the *Oxford Magazine* and the *Town and Country Magazine*, were illustrated with satirical prints. The sales of most of these publications would be higher than that for the majority of those political caricatures which appeared as individual prints. The *Public Advertiser*, for example, usually sold more than 2,000 copies per issue in the late 1760s and sales never dropped below 3,000 copies in the 1770s.[4] Illustrations of this kind occasionally reached a vast audience in the early nineteenth century. George Cruikshank was enormously successful in his collaborations with William Hone, the radical publisher. In 1819 Hone produced a twenty-four page pamphlet, *The House that Jack Built*, which sold for one shilling, the price of a single print. This pamphlet was illustrated by a dozen small prints which Cruikshank engraved in boxwood, a technique that Thomas Bewick brought to perfection. *The House that Jack Built* reached fifty editions by the end of 1820 and sold some 100,000 copies.[5] Since most pamphlets were read by many more people than the purchaser, Cruikshank must have reached a huge audience. In 1820 Cruikshank produced *The Man in the Moon* (*113*) as an illustration for a verse satire produced by William Hone. By 1821 this had reached its fifty-first edition and perhaps emulated the sales of *The House that Jack Built*.[6] The ability to produce low-cost illustrated periodicals and pamphlets, by means of wood engravings and lithographs rather than copper engravings, marked the sharp decline of the independent caricature print, but it greatly increased the market for political illustrations and cartoons. By the early 1830s two of the most active professional caricaturists, William Heath and Robert Seymour, were illustrating *The Looking Glass* and the *Monthly Sheet of Caricatures*, both of which were produced by Thomas McLean, the leading printseller in London.[7]

The indications are therefore that most political prints appealed to a relatively limited audience, but that a minority did succeed in reaching a mass market. In social

* Italicised numbers in the text refer to the plates in this volume. Numbers prefaced with BMC refer to catalogue numbers in the British Museum *Catalogue of Political and Personal Satires*.

and geographical terms, too, most political prints usually reached only a restricted market, but occasionally they had a much wider appeal. Nearly all the political prints were produced and sold in London and Westminster. The prints were largely designed for an urban market, mainly a metropolitan market. In the later eighteenth century the cost of purchasing a print was usually sixpence plain and one shilling coloured. By the early nineteenth century the cost was often double these rates. These prices were well beyond the means of the lower orders and even the lower middle classes in the provinces must have found it prohibitively expensive to purchase regular supplies of prints from the capital. In the late 1780s and early 1790s some printsellers, including William Holland and Samuel Fores, organised exhibitions of prints and charged an entrance fee of one shilling. Fores also lent out folios of caricatures for the evening and organised a circulating library for prints and drawings, but these schemes must still have been beyond the financial means of the lower orders.[8] Moreover, while it is true that there are several contemporary references to crowds gathering outside the shops of printsellers in London, attracted there by the opportunity of freely perusing the prints in the windows, it needs to be remembered that there were fewer than ten such shops and they were all in central London. They could hardly have attracted huge numbers to their windows. There are other indications to suggest that most prints were not perused by the lower orders. Many prints included some writing and most political prints assumed a high level of political intelligence and knowledge. The prints themselves were preoccupied with the actions and lifestyles of the propertied classes. Only a minority paid any attention to the labouring poor and, when they did so, they invariably portrayed them as ignorant, rapacious and irresponsible. Most prints therefore reached a metropolitan and prosperous audience, but there clearly were exceptions to this general rule. At times of political crisis efforts were made by both radicals and conservatives to reach the lower orders. As we shall see below, several political organisations subsidised the cost of producing political prints so that they could be sold more cheaply. Samuel Fores offered reduced rates per one hundred copies of a print to those who wished to give them away.[9] When the middle classes feared revolution they pasted political prints on the walls of taverns, shops and workshops in an effort to influence the lower orders. At times therefore some prints were perused by large numbers of the labouring poor.

2. POLITICIANS AND CARICATURES

Although political prints, unlike newspapers, did not have a mass circulation throughout the nation at large, they did often reach a significant proportion of the middling orders of the metropolis and occasionally did appeal to a very large audience. It is certainly evident that the governing classes believed that the prints could have a considerable impact on responsible public opinion, that is on the middling orders in the metropolis and other large urban areas. The Prince Regent, later George IV, not only built up a large collection of prints, but also betrayed considerable fear about being personally ridiculed by caricaturists. In 1820, when he was the target for a host of prints attacking him for putting his wife on trial, he tried to prevent the appearance of grossly offensive caricatures by the suppression of individual plates. He bought up the plate and copyright, including any impressions already printed, from the printseller who undertook not to publish anything else on the same subject. Robert Cruikshank was paid £70 and George Cruikshank £100 'in consideration of a pledge not to caricature His Majesty in any immoral situation'. This tactic was fraught with difficulty. The pledge was too easily evaded by an anonymous print and blackmail was encouraged. Lewis Marks, who was paid more than any other caricaturist for suppressing prints against the King, appears to have been a brazen blackmailer. The records reveal no less than ten separate transactions between Marks and George IV in 1820.[10] Charles James Fox and Robert Peel, both favourite subjects of the caricaturists, also built up fine collections of prints. Clearly, as is the case today, there were some politicians who sought publicity and who enjoyed having a high public profile, even if they were subjected to more criticism than praise. The young George Canning was particularly keen to see himself caricatured in print and, through an intermediary, urged James Gillray to portray him in one of his productions.[11]

Those interested in the state of public opinion were not preoccupied solely with their own personal appearance in the prints. They clearly recognised the political impact of the prints and endeavoured to enlist the best caricaturists in their propaganda campaigns. In 1766 Edmund Burke, private secretary to the Prime Minister, the Marquis of Rockingham, and Grey Cooper, the secretary to the Treasury, urged Benjamin Wilson to produce a print in support of the repeal of the Stamp Act. The result was the immensely popular *The Repeal, Or, the Funeral of Miss Ame-Stamp* (9).[12] William Pitt, the Younger, rewarded James Sayers, the major rival to James Gillray, with sinecure posts as rewards for his potent jibes at Charles James Fox in his caricature prints of 1783 and 1784.[13] Fox was reported later as having said that 'Sayers's caricatures had done him more mischief than the debates in Parliament or the works of the press'.[14] Gillray was also commissioned by the Pitt camp and produced seven anti-Foxite plates during the Westminster election of 1784. He was to be paid £20 for his services, a sum which may not have been paid because, after the election, Gillray attacked Pitt's efforts to bribe the voters. In 1788 the ministry again hired Gillray, this time to support Admiral Hood's campaign for re-election at Westminster following his appointment as First Lord of the Admiralty. Gillray produced seven prints, all among his worst, and then produced two more effective prints savagely attacking Hood's electioneering tactics.[15] Gillray was clearly not averse to biting the hand that fed him.

In the 1790s, when there was an extremely sharp political division between radicals and conservatives, considerably greater efforts were made to enlist the best caricaturists into the political debate. The Association for the Preservation of Liberty and Property against Republicans and Levellers, a loyalist and reactionary organisation established with government support by John Reeves, subsidised prints against Jacobin subversion. The Association subsidised two of Thomas Rowlandson's prints in December 1792. *The Contrast* (BMC 8149) and *Philosophy Run Mad or a Stupendous Monument of Human Wisdom* (BMC 8150) sold for threepence plain, sixpence coloured, or one guinea or two guineas per hundred. The Association was singled out for praise in 1792 by James Sayers in his *Loyalty against Levelling* (BMC 8138) and by Isaac Cruikshank(?) in 1794 in *A Picture of Great Britain in the Year 1793* (56). Other caricaturists joined in the anti-Jacobin campaign of their own volition. James Gillray shared in the widespread fear of revolution, but, at least at first, he was contemptuous of Reeves and his supporters who met at the Crown and Anchor tavern in London. His print, *John Bull Bother'd* (BMC 8141), is inscribed 'Price 3 shills.ˢ— The engraving not having been Paid for, by the associations for vending two penny Scurrilities'.[16] In January 1795, however, at the height of the reaction against the British Jacobins, Gillray produced *The Blessings of Peace. The Curses of War* (BMC 8609) for 'The Chairman and Members of the Crown & Anchor Society'. It appears that Gillray failed to receive satisfactory compensation for his services. When Reeves was subsequently criticised by the House of Commons for an alleged libel on the constitution, Gillray ridiculed him in *The Crown & Anchor Libel* (BMC 8699). In November 1795, he dedicated this print 'To the Chairman & Members of the truly Loyal Association at the Crown and Anchor' as a 'small token of Gratitude for favors receiv'd'.[17] Gillray had a similarly unfortunate experience in 1798 when Sir John Dalrymple set on foot a scheme for publishing below cost price a set of twenty large plates by Gillray on the subject of *The Consequences of a Successful French Invasion*. Dalrymple invited private subscriptions, but also counted upon Treasury support which he failed to get. Gillray produced only four of the plates (BMC 9180–3) before the scheme foundered.[18]

At ministerial level George Canning was more highly sensitive to the value of prints in shaping public opinion than was any other politician. Through an intermediary, the Rev. John Sneyd, he established contact with James Gillray, the most successful caricaturist of the day, in the autumn of 1795. In 1796 he may have assisted Gillray when he was arrested for a print ridiculing the Prince of Wales. The charges were certainly dropped. A secret pension of perhaps £200 p.a. was subsequently paid to Gillray from December 1797. This pension lapsed in 1801 when Addington became Prime Minister, but it may have been resumed in 1807 or 1808. In return for his pension Gillray became a more convinced supporter of the Pittites and a determined opponent of the Foxite Whigs. In November 1797 Canning initiated the *Anti-Jacobin*, a weekly journal of news and satire including a weekly examination of the 'Lies, Misrepresentations and Mistakes' committed by the opposition press. Gillray produced four prints for the *Anti-Jacobin*, the most famous being *The Friend of Humanity and the Knife-Grinder* (BMC 9045) which appeared in December 1797. This did not win the complete admiration of his patrons, however, since Gillray turned what had been intended as a general satire on the self-proclaimed 'Friends of Humanity' into a personal satire on George Tierney, the Foxite M.P. for Southwark. The *Anti-Jacobin*, although a considerable success, only lasted eight months before its last edition in July 1798. Gillray did contribute six plates to its successor, the monthly *Anti-Jacobin Review and Magazine*, which started up in July 1798. In 1799 three new editions of the original *Anti-Jacobin* were published. In 1800 a de luxe edition of the *Poetry of the Anti-Jacobin* was planned and Gillray was hired to produce the illustrations. Canning and his friends soon became concerned at the prospect that Gillray would produce a series of personal caricatures as illustrations instead of generalised moral satires. After several months of work by Gillray the project was abandoned, though Canning did pay Gillray £150 to compensate him for the destruction of the plates which he had already completed. In 1806 Canning again turned to Gillray for assistance in the propaganda campaign against the Whig-dominated Ministry of all the Talents. Gillray produced some twenty-five political satires over a period of sixteen months in which he attacked the divisions, greed, egotism and self-interest of this administration.[19]

It was not only the supporters of the government or the political elite who encouraged or subsidised the production of political prints. Several newspapers and periodicals published opposition or radical prints in the late 1760s and early 1770s. The famous attack on Bute's destruction of the constitution, *Samson pulling down the Pillars* (10), appeared in John Almon's *Political Register* in 1767, while *Hercules cleaning the Augean Stable* (BMC 4186) appeared in 1768. A few prints were subsidised directly by radical societies. *A Cure for National Grievances* (55), which was probably published in 1793, was described as being produced for 'Citizen Lee, at the British Tree of Liberty, 98 Berwick Street, Soho'. It sold for one penny, which was clearly under cost price and it was clearly directed to the attention of the lower orders. In the 1820s four radical publishers, Benbow, Carlile, Dolby and Hone, all published radical prints, while John Fairburn was a leading seller of such prints.[20] George Cruikshank, the leading caricaturist of his day, was prepared to produce political prints at the instigation of both radical and conservative publishers. As we have already seen he collaborated most successfully with the radical publisher, William Hone, on *The Political House that Jack Built* and on *The Man in the Moon* (113). At the same time, in 1820–1 he was paid to produce caricature prints hostile to the reformers and to their leaders in particular. He contributed ten anti-reform caricatures to *The Loyalists' Magazine*, a Tory weekly, and he also produced the frontispiece to a Tory pamphlet, *The Radical Chiefs*.[21]

3. THE ART OF THE CARICATURISTS

Both active politicians and committed radicals clearly believed that political prints could serve a propaganda purpose and they were prepared to hire professional artists to engrave satires to order. Other political activists, who were particularly anxious to influence public opinion, produced their own prints. Large numbers of prints were produced by amateurs who only engraved a single plate on a political topic which excited their interest. Political prints were not just produced by political activists who wanted to shape public opinion towards a specific end however. A growing proportion of prints was produced in order to sell at a profit to a public already involved in a political issue or ready to be interested in a whole range of issues. The production of political prints remained largely under amateur control in the middle decades of the eighteenth century, but, from the 1780s, professional artists began to dominate the medium of graphic satire. A small number of professionals not only set the tone of, but produced a high proportion of political prints in, the great age of caricature in the late eighteenth and early nineteenth centuries. Many amateurs continued to produce a single print or two, but it was the small body of professional artists who catered for the mass market in the capital and other urban centres. From the 1790s onwards almost three quarters of all prints that were produced were the work of the half dozen leading artists of the day. The market demand was met by a few caricaturists working full time on the production of prints. The most gifted artists – James Gillray, Thomas Rowlandson, James Sayers and George Cruikshank – were joined by such able craftsmen as William Dent, William Heath, Robert Seymour, Isaac Cruikshank and John Doyle (who used the initials HB). At the same time there was a rise in the number of specialist printshops in London and Westminster, though in this case too the market was supplied by a small number of printsellers.[22] The most active included William, George and Hannah Humphrey, Matthew and Mary Darly, Samuel Fores, William Holland and Thomas McLean.[23]

Both the professional caricaturists and the specialist printsellers were, for the most part, drawn from the lower middle classes and they aimed to reach a large middle class market with their wares. Although both were ready to produce prints to order they were also conscious of the need to respond to political events which were already exciting public interest in order to secure a steady income. Political crises undoubtedly sold prints, but professional printmakers and sellers could not always afford to wait upon events. They tried to find, perhaps even to manufacture, subjects upon which they might comment. They read newspapers and periodicals, listened to parliamentary debates and sought out political gossip in order to find topics which they could make relevant and interesting to a large body of opinion. Most professional printmakers did not produce prints solely on those political issues about which they had decided views of their own. They not only hired out their skills, but also tailored their comments to different audiences or to the changing moods of the same audience. They were prepared to attack quite indiscriminately such political rivals as Pitt and Fox or Wellington and Grey. Artists of the calibre of James Gillray and George Cruikshank were frequently highly critical of corruption in high places and of the misuse of government power and yet they were also often hostile to those who campaigned for radical reforms. This behaviour may have reflected their own rather ambivalent attitudes, but it is difficult to avoid the conclusion that they were conscious of the views and prejudices of the potential buyers of political prints. Sometimes the professional caricaturists tried to instruct their audience what to think about a political issue. More often they encapsulated public opinion and fed this back to the political elite who dominated the decision-making processes of the state. Sensitivity to the public mood was necessary for professional survival. Successful caricaturists had therefore to cater for as many different shades of opinion as possible. They learned to veil their own opinions under layers of cynicism and irony. Nonetheless, even in providing a large public with what it wanted, they increased public knowledge of political issues and helped to create a larger market for subsequent political prints.

Whether he was an amateur seeking to explain his own political convictions to the public or a professional hired by political activists or simply hoping to reap a commercial profit from his artistic ability, the printmaker set out to win a wide response and to influence a significant body of opinion. In order to be successful political prints, whether designed as conscious propaganda or commercial ventures, had to be popular. In seeking maximum impact and in endeavouring to reach as large a market as possible the printmakers of the late eighteenth and early nineteenth centuries were consistently attempting to improve their skills and to popularise their craft. The traditional emblematic or 'hieroglyphic' style of engraving, with its intricate and complicated message, its involved symbolism and its explanatory verses or keys, gradually gave way to bolder and simpler designs which had a more immediate appeal to the eye. In the 1770s Matthew Darly and his wife, Mary, led the way in the new methods of producing prints. Coloured versions of prints became increasingly common. Light etching, which allows for more flowing freedom in design and execution, began to replace deeper engraving by the late eighteenth century. By the 1820s lithography and wood engraving began to challenge the supremacy of etchings and copper engravings. Throughout the whole period political prints were dominated by the caricature in which personalised political attacks were made through artistic distortion. The character and appearance of public figures were exaggerated in a burlesque or grotesque way. In political caricatures wit, satire and scurrility, violence, sex and even pornography were all used to produce a dramatic design and immediate visual impact. Coarse imagery, earthy vulgarity and savage humour were well suited to the critical purpose of most prints. Only very occasionally did political prints bestow compliments or defend particular positions. They were more effective when they employed ridicule or aroused hate. There were many more prints which attacked government ministers than defended them. By the same token there were many more criticisms of radicals than there were indications of support for their political aims.

Political prints were persuasive precisely because their imagery was vivid and concrete. They were powerful as weapons of personal satire and as a medium for expressing complex issues in a direct and simple form. Political prints argued by assertion, appealed to authority and prejudice, and relied heavily upon shibboleths and rhetoric. Virtues and vices were depicted most effectively when they were given human or animal form. Liberty was portrayed as a woman with a cap and pole, Justice carried her sword and scales, while Britannia bore a shield and spear. John Bull came to personify England and the English. Portrayed occasionally as a bull (*36, 60, 78, 97*), but more often as a burly squire or citizen of simple manners and hearty appetites (*63, 80, 84, 127, 148*), he was the personification of independence, courage, patriotism and stoicism. Animals of various kinds appeared in the prints to represent particular human qualities: asses personified stupidity, lions valour, serpents guile, bulldogs resolution and foxes treachery. Some public figures were occasionally given animal form to heighten the satire. Charles James Fox was, not surprisingly, depicted as a fox in many prints. Francis Burdett was occasionally a goose (e.g. BMC 10732) and William Cobbett a porcupine (*81, 83*). The unpopular Earl of Bute appeared as a jackboot in a great many prints (*3*). Political dangers were also expressed in concrete form. The threat posed by arbitrary power was often made vivid and manifest in huge monsters and seven-headed hydras (*4, 13, 33, 57, 61, 71, 80, 88, 135*). Devils, demons and imps were employed to suggest subversion (*109, 110, 134, 144*), while gaping chasms and jaws of hell warned of the dangers of revolution (*146*). Political institutions were also given visual form. The constitution was frequently represented as a temple or some kind of structure (*10, 11, 22, 56, 68, 114*), while the state was often depicted as a ship (*53*). The enemies of the constitution were generally portrayed as trampling on Magna Carta, the Bill of Rights and Habeas Corpus (*7*). On the other hand, anything which could not easily be satirised, simplified or rendered concrete for dramatic visual effect was largely ignored by the caricaturists. Constitutional theories and radical ideology, which were much debated in the press, were treated only superficially in the prints. The dangers of revolution were often depicted, but the caricaturists found it difficult to portray the benefits of reform or the organisations by which political changes might be achieved.

Because of its inability to express complex political programmes the political caricature never attained the aura of authority and veracity associated with the printed word. Those in power did not usually regard political prints as highly dangerous weapons in the hands of the disaffected. They were only occasionally used by extreme radicals in any case. The prints were generally produced by the respectable middle classes for moderate public opinion. As a consequence they enjoyed more tolerance than the printed word, especially in times of political crisis. The prints were not subject to stamp duty in the same way as newspapers and pamphlets and they were hardly ever prosecuted for seditious libel. This licence was partly because the governing elite did not wish to give additional publicity to scurrilous prints and, in part, because they were not confident that they could secure a conviction against a subversive caricature as easily as against the printed word; but it was also because political prints reached a more restricted market, both socially and geographically, than radical newspapers and pamphlets and because the most effective caricaturists while often critical of government were not subversive. They ridiculed the failings of the governing elite, but they did not endorse popular revolution or radical constitutional reforms. Most caricatures spoke to and for that respectable body of opinion which wanted to redress grievances but not to turn the world upside down.

II.
The Prints and the Constitution

The strengths and weaknesses of political prints as both comments and influences upon political questions are clearly seen in a study of how the caricaturists responded to the debate over the constitution in the late eighteenth and early nineteenth centuries. Political prints appeared on all aspects of the debate about the constitution. They reveal why the constitution was defended and also why it was attacked, but they were not equally effective on all aspects of the debate. They found it difficult to explain the precise virtues of the constitution, though they made a powerful case against those who wished to reform it. The caricaturists also found it easier to illustrate the grievances against which reformers campaigned than to explain the positive aims and the political methods of those reformers. While the prints undervalued the impact of the American Revolution and the Industrial Revolution on the constitutional debate, they quite clearly reveal the enormous impact of the French Revolution on political opinion in Britain. Although the prints are a superb source for the influence of major personalities on the constitutional debate, they seriously underestimate the impact of political organisations. The caricaturists surprisingly neglected the many efforts to reform the constitution before 1830, but they are a magnificent source on almost every aspect of the great debate on the constitution between 1829 and the final passing of the Reform Bill in 1832.

1. THE DEFENCE OF THE CONSTITUTION

By the mid-eighteenth century most of the political nation and indeed the majority of the lower orders too were convinced that the British constitution was the finest in the world. The constitution was almost universally praised for its ability to achieve the twin goals of good government: namely, liberty and authority. Britain appeared to enjoy the benefits of mixed government, through the judicious combination of monarchy, aristocracy and democracy, which secured the benefits of each type of government in its pure form while avoiding their particular disadvantages. Monarchy in its pure form avoided disputes over who could exercise authority and this allowed the sovereign to act promptly in an emergency; but it placed the liberty and property of the subject at the mercy of one man who might decide to act as an arbitrary tyrant. Aristocracy provided an able elite capable of leading and offering an inspiring example to the nation, but it too often degenerated into a narrow oligarchy of warring, self-interested factions. Democracy offered the greatest degree of liberty to the ordinary subject, but it was too slow to act and was so inherently unstable that it invariably soon collapsed into anarchy or mob rule. On the other hand, a mixed form of government maximised the constraints upon power and prevented its abuse, whilst also ensuring that the people enjoyed as much liberty as was compatible with political stability. The benefits of mixed government were achieved in practice by the balanced constitution of King, Lords and Commons. Each of these institutions had its own peculiar privileges and distinct functions. As chief magistrate the king was above the law, was the fount of honour, was the unchallenged head of the executive and retained various prerogative powers including the right to summon, prorogue and dissolve parliament. The aristocracy enjoyed the highest honours of the state, sat in the upper chamber of parliament as of right, and formed the highest court of justice in the land. The members of the House of Commons were the representatives of the people and, as such, they were charged with the task of defending the liberties of the subject against, and laying the grievances of the subject before, the executive. They also enjoyed the privilege of initiating all taxes. In addition to these distinct functions all three institutions – King, Lords and Commons – combined to form the sovereign legislature. No bill could become law unless it was approved by all three branches of the legislature in the same session of parliament. There was no distinct separation of powers even though the king dominated the executive, the House of Lords was the supreme court of justice, and the House of Commons initiated revenue-raising bills. The executive and the judiciary interacted with the legislature and the sovereign legislature was a combination of King, Lords and Commons. The constitution was therefore a complicated system of checks and balances. It preserved the privileges peculiar to the monarch, the nobility and the people, whilst also endeavouring to secure a harmonious relationship between all three. It was this delicate balance and equilibrium which attracted so much admiration and which was the object of so much jealous concern in case the constitution was unbalanced and its manifest benefits lost.[24]

A great many political caricaturists evidently admired this constitution and wished to preserve it from subversion from within or assault from without, but they found it very difficult to depict the virtues of the constitution in their prints. The complicated relationship of King, Lords and Commons was almost impossible to represent in visual form. Some caricaturists depicted the constitution as a temple, which was supported by three pillars inscribed with the words King, Lords and Commons. This is the case in *Samson pulling down the Pillars* (10) and *A Picture of Great Britain in the Year 1793* (56). In *The Contrast, or things as they are* (BMC 8834) the constitution was portrayed as a triangle supported by the three pillars of King, Lords and Commons. A more elaborate attempt to explain the merits of the constitution was made by the engraver of *The Palace of John Bull* (114). On the dome of his temple he had Britannia placing the statue of Liberty and within the temple the king was enthroned between Justice and a parson. In *The Constitution of England* (22) it was three sturdy tree trunks which were labelled King, Lords and Commons. These tree trunks supported a pair of scales in which were balanced religion, law and authority on one side against liberty, right and obedience on the other. In many other prints the virtues of the British

24

constitution were alluded to by such inscriptions as 'Magna Carta', 'Bill of Rights' and 'Habeas Corpus'. A classic example of this approach is *The Vision or M—n–st–l Monster; address'd to the Friends of Old England* (4).

Those who wished to defend the constitution against its critics constantly referred to the positive benefits which the nation had reaped since the Glorious Revolution of 1688. The constitution was credited with saving the country from absolutism and with inaugurating a period of unparalleled liberty, social stability and economic advance. By ensuring the rule of law the constitution preserved civil liberties and protected private property from the twin dangers of arbitrary tyranny and mob rule. When James Gillray wished to portray the Younger Pitt as the trusted defender of the constitution against all its enemies, he produced a print, *Britannia between Scylla and Charybdis* (53), which showed the Prime Minister steering the ship of the constitution between the rock of democracy and the whirlpool of arbitrary power. Other caricaturists also feared that the constitution was in danger from both ministerial tyranny and mob rule. George Cruikshank, in *Hunt-ing the Bull* (97), showed John Bull pursued by both a radical mob and a number of ministerial butchers, while Robert Seymour, in *John Bull's Night Mare* (121), showed a sick John Bull beset by both ministers and radicals. In the late eighteenth and early nineteenth centuries, however, nearly all the defenders of the constitution saw the major threat coming from the forces of democracy. It was the critics of the constitution who feared the threat posed by executive power. In seeking to defend the constitution therefore its supporters concentrated their fire on those who wished to reduce the power of the executive and to increase the power of the legislature and of the people at large.

The conservative defenders of the constitution condemned the characters, the aims and the methods of those who advocated reforms in the direction of greater accountability of those in power. The leading reformers and radicals were invariably attacked as ambitious men posing as disinterested patriots, as foolish men putting forward impractical schemes, or as dangerous fanatics plotting violent revolution. Hogarth's famous satire on John Wilkes (6) portrayed the self-proclaimed patriot as the embodiment of cunning and impudent demagogy. In this print the cap and staff of liberty are sardonic symbols. To his supporters Charles James Fox was the champion of the people, but to his critics his patriotism masked dangerous political ambitions. In *The Mirror of Patriotism* (32) James Sayers depicted Fox standing before a mirror in which the reflection was that of Cromwell in armour. In *The Republican Soldier!* (BMC 9204) Isaac Cruikshank portrays Fox as a soldier plotting rebellion, while in *A Right Hon. Democrat Dissected* (52) William Dent accused Fox of every possible personal and political vice. In *John Bull consulting the Oracle!* (72) James Gillray warned John Bull to reject Fox's claim that radical reform would save him from misery, ruin and debt, while in *The Tree of Liberty – With the Devil Tempting John Bull* (74) he instructed John Bull that the fruit of the reforms proffered to him by Fox would be murder, plunder and revolution. Several radicals were accused of putting forward fantastic and impractical schemes which ought to be rejected with contempt. In

Fashion before Ease; – Or, – A good Constitution sacrificed for a Fantastick Form (51) James Gillray ridiculed Paine's efforts to force a buxom Britannia into a pair of stays which he is drawing dangerously tight. In *Radical Quacks giving a new Constitution to John Bull (118)* George Cruikshank shows John Bull, with his legs amputated by means of universal suffrage and religious freedom, being bled by Francis Burdett and offered further dangerous remedies. In *The Smithfield Parliament i.e. Universal Suffrage – The New Speaker Addressing the Members (105)* Henry Hunt, with the head of an ass, addresses an audience of cattle, sheep, horses and pigs, all on their hind legs. Most radicals however are treated as revolutionary fanatics rather than as impractical fools. In the 1790s Joseph Priestley, Richard Price and Thomas Paine were all portrayed in numerous prints as plotters conspiring to destroy the constitution in church and state by violent means. Typical of these savage indictments is Isaac Cruikshank's *The Friends of the People (49)*. Caricatures condemning reformers as revolutionary conspirators were once again common in the crisis years of 1815 to 1820. One of the most famous was George Cruikshank's *The Radical Ladder (119)* which shows Queen Caroline and the radical leaders mounting a ladder of violent protests that was leading to anarchy and revolution. The worst fears of the anti-reformers were confirmed by the Cato Street conspiracy which was the subject of several prints: e.g. *(115)*.

Although the caricaturists depicted individual radicals more often than radical organisations, whenever they took notice of the latter they almost always did so in order to attack them. Extra-parliamentary organisations were clearly regarded by most caricaturists as subversive threats to duly constituted authority. In *A Petitioning, Remonstrating, Reforming, Republican (29)* the Associators of 1780 were accused of supporting rebellion not liberty. The Society for Constitutional Information, the greatest disseminator of radical propaganda, was lampooned by James Sayers as an ass, laden with radical works, braying the 'Rights of Man' and kicking out at the British lion. Sayers gave this print the ironically misleading title *Published by Order of the Society for Constitutional Information by D. A[dam]s Secret^y (44)*, but he added the inscription 'From all Seditions privy Conspiracy and Rebellion from all false Doctrine Heresy and Schism &c. Good Lord deliver us'. The Revolution Society was condemned in *A Birmingham Toast* (BMC 7894) for drinking toasts against the king, the Norwich radicals were condemned 'for their readiness to sacrifice their country to French interests (BMC 8617), while the London Corresponding Society was represented as a gang of brutal and impoverished conspirators *(73)*. The destruction of the radical societies in the late 1790s was met with approval by the caricaturists (see BMC 9230, 9258 and 9345). Even the moderate Foxite Whigs, who were a group of wealthy parliamentarians, were libelled in many prints for supposedly endorsing revolutionary principles. In *Parliamentary Reform – Or – Opposition Rats leaving the House they had undermined (69)* the seceding Foxites are shown as rats deserting the House of Commons after the failure of their motion for parliamentary reform in 1797. In *The Loyal Toast* (BMC 9168) the Duke of Norfolk is portrayed leading the Foxites in a toast to 'Our Sovereign, – the Majesty of the People'.

The conservative defenders of the constitution in the 1790s accused both the leading reformers and all the radical organisations of preparing the way for a French invasion and the forcible introduction of French revolutionary principles. In *A Peace Offering to the Genius of Liberty and Property* (57) Isaac Cruikshank portrayed the leading Foxite Whigs as sansculottes laying offerings before a hideous woman representing republican liberty. James Gillray's *Patriotic Regeneration – Viz. – Parliament Reform'd, a la Francoise* (59) depicted the Foxites as sansculottes who have taken over the House of Commons by force. Numerous prints warn the nation of the horrors which would befall it should its cherished constitution ever be exchanged for the French model. Violence, tyranny and poverty would be the immediate results. (See, for example, BMC 8145, 8288, 8289, 8834, 9055 and 9369.) The tyranny of the people would be far worse than the most determined despotism of any European monarch.

To the defenders of the constitution reform would destroy individual liberty, private property, the established Church and all order in the state. Even moderate reforms would soon lead to the establishment of a democratic form of government that would prove to be more unstable and more corrupt than any other form of government. In democracies all subordination was destroyed and the voice of reason was drowned by the clamour of violence and fanatic enthusiasm. To give the vote to the unpropertied classes would be to entrust power to the most passionate, irresponsible and violent of men. Should such men ever be in a position to influence the decisions of the legislature then all order would be subverted and anarchy would prevail. Political reform would prove to be the first step to social revolution. The sovereignty of the people, once unleashed, would not be content to eliminate corruption and safeguard the liberty of the subject. The licentious mob would attack all privileges, including all social and economic distinctions, and it would make a determined effort to remedy what the poor regarded as the greatest grievance in society, namely the unequal distribution of property. An equality of political rights would be followed by demands for an equality of possessions.

Such fears as these are clearly present in many political prints. The reformers and radicals are frequently portrayed not only as the enemies of church and state (e.g. BMC 7628–30), but also as the bringers of chaos and terror. One of the most dramatic prints of this latter kind is George Cruikshank's *A Radical Reformer – A Neck or Nothing Man* (108). Several caricaturists associated radical political reform with dangerous social ambitions of the lower orders. Radicals were frequently portrayed as fierce, ugly, irresponsible and ragged members of the lower classes. James Gillray's *London Corresponding Society, Alarm'd* (73) shows a small group of brutal, ragged men. Samuel de Wilde's *The Robbing Hood Debating Society* (82) depicts a ruffianly gang of radicals, some of whom are pick-pockets working for the speaker on the rostrum. The same engraver's *The Reformers Dinner* (BMC 11335) portrays most of the guests as disreputable characters. Two prints portray mass meetings of radicals and both depict the radicals as ragged, ugly, brutal characters. James Gillray's *Copenhagen House* (62) shows one of the huge crowds addressed by John Thelwall in 1795, while

George Cruikshank's *The Belle Alliance or the Female Reformers of Blackburn* (106) combines the social threat with a sexual threat in his print of lower class female radicals supporting their menfolk in 1819. Cruikshank's *Universal Suffrage, Or – The Scum Uppermost* (104) was even more direct. In this print the many-headed monster is destroying monarchy, justice and liberty.

In parliamentary speeches and in the press the conservatives offered effective criticisms of all the various plans put forward to reform the constitution. Political conservatives defended the crown's ability to influence the composition of both houses of parliament by means of the skilful distribution of honours, offices and financial rewards. Royal patronage was an essential balance to parliament's greater influence over the voting of taxes. Mixed government could not survive unless the crown used its patronage to build up a body of supporters in parliament who would protect its interests there. Conservative spokesmen also challenged all the arguments which reformers put forward in support of a reform of the electoral system. They argued that any extension of the franchise would only swamp the opinions of responsible men of property with the violent and uncontrolled passions of the ignorant masses. A redistribution of parliamentary constituencies would either give the landed interest too much influence if the counties secured greater representation or would subvert the landed interest if the large towns were given increased representation. Frequent general elections would only increase the opportunities for dissipation, tumult and corruption and would force Members of Parliament to spend more time nursing their constituencies than serving the nation. Members would either strive to be popular with their constituents or would succumb to tempting offers from the administration which would help them with their electoral expenses. In either case they would pursue selfish ends or sectional interests to the exclusion of the public interest. The consequence would be either perpetual instability as Members of Parliament bowed to popular pressure and refused to take difficult decisions or a House of Commons entirely corrupted by the Court. Both liberty and stability would then be lost. To abolish property qualifications for parliamentary candidates and to pay Members of Parliament would encourage ill-educated and self-educated demagogues to compete for election with men who possessed the necessary wealth, education and leisure to be trusted with the fate of the nation. None of these sophisticated intellectual arguments against parliamentary reform or against any scheme to curtail the patronage of the crown made their way into the political prints. The caricaturists could express hate or fear of the reformers and could point out the dangers of revolution, but they were incapable of destroying the intellectual foundations of the reformers' arguments. Instead, they incited fear and occasionally rejoiced in the repressive measures taken against the radicals. In *The Tree of Liberty must be planted immediately* (BMC 8986) James Gillray urged, no doubt tongue in cheek, that liberty could best be preserved if the Foxites and the radicals were beheaded. Two years later, in 1799, he was approving of the investigations of radical activities by the Secret Committee of the House of Commons which endorsed repressive policies against the reformers. Isaac Cruikshank's famous print, *The Royal Extinguisher or Gulliver putting out the Patriots of Lilliput* (*64*), evidently approved of Pitt's attempts to silence the insignificant radicals meeting in Copenhagen Fields. A generation later, in 1821, his son, George Cruikshank, imitated his father's print with *The Royal Extinguisher, Or the King of Brobdingnag & the Lilliputians* (BMC 14145). In this print it is George IV who is about to put a big extinguisher over Queen Caroline and her radical supporters.

2. CRITICISMS OF THE CONSTITUTION

In the middle decades of the eighteenth century there were few critics of the fundamental principles which underlay the British constitution. With the exception of a small number of extreme Jacobites almost all the critics of successive administrations joined those in power in upholding the virtues of the rule of law and in praising the merits of mixed government and the balanced constitution. These critics – Tory, Country and Patriot alike – praised the principles of the constitution, but they protested vociferously that these principles were being undermined in practice by the seductive influence of power, place and money. They accused a narrow oligarchy of monopolising office and of exploiting the patronage of the crown and the power and financial resources of the executive in order to undermine the independence of the legislature and hence threaten the liberty of the subject. Opposition critics claimed that the level of taxation, of the national debt, and of the civil list and the size of the armed forces, the court and the government bureaucracy were all being increased in order to provide the patronage and financial inducements needed to persuade Members of Parliament and humble voters alike to sacrifice the interests of the nation for their own personal and material advancement. It was thus maintained, vigorously and repeatedly, that the Court had gained so much power to influence the electorate and Members of Parliament that the balanced constitution was in serious danger. In the past, these critics insisted, the crown had attempted to subvert parliament by a direct assault upon its privileges and authority. These attacks had been successfully repulsed. By the more surreptitious and insidious use of crown patronage, however, the Court could now control the composition of parliament and weaken both the aristocratic and the democratic elements of the constitution. The balanced constitution of King, Lords and Commons might continue to exist in theory, but, in practice, the first was in the process of acquiring an unconstitutional power over the other two. If the constitution were to be saved and the liberties of the subject protected then the advance of crown patronage and the corrupt practices of the narrow oligarchy in office must be first halted and subsequently reversed.

The attacks on crown patronage and executive corruption, which were being voiced in parliament in the early Hanoverian period, were launched by all elements of the extra-parliamentary opposition of the late eighteenth and early nineteenth centuries. Christopher Wyvill and the Association Movement led the rural and metropolitan middle classes in denunciation of such abuses. Thomas Paine and William Cobbett, both of whom reached huge numbers of the lower orders, warned of the political and social consequences of government patronage and corruption. The political caricaturists found these abuses to be large and irresistible targets for their satire. All the leading ministers of the period were subjected to the charge that they were endangering the constitution and the liberty of the subject with their corrupt practices. The Earl of Bute was frequently condemned for monopolising crown patronage and for using it to enlist impoverished, dependent Scotsmen in his cause. This is the burden of the satire in *The Caledonians Arrival in Money-Land* (2). In *The Colossus of the North; or the Striding Boreas* (23) Lord North is shown striding across a stream down which float a large number of M.P.s. The Prime Minister stands upon two blocks which are inscribed with the words 'Tyranny' and 'Venality', while in one hand he holds papers labelled 'Places', 'Pensions' and 'Lottery Tickets'. The Younger Pitt and his main agent for the distribution of patronage, Henry Dundas, were the targets for many savage caricatures. In *The End of Parliament* (36) William Dent drew a snorting bull collapsing under an enormous load of taxes; while Pitt and Dundas pull a chain of loaves and fishes from the bull's posterior. James Gillray's *A New Way to Pay the National Debt* (35) shows Pitt, with George III and the Queen, at the Treasury distributing money and places to hordes of soldiers and placemen. There are over thirty prints violently attacking Dundas during the years 1805–7 when he was under investigation for frauds and irregularities while in office. Even more dramatic was the scandal which erupted in 1809 when it became known that the Duke of York's mistress was in a position to sell commissions in the army. Over one hundred caricatures appeared on this subject. Even after 1815, when efforts were being made to reduce the size of the military establishment and the civil service, there were numerous attacks on the burden which the executive placed on the subject in its efforts to safeguard its patronage. In 1819 George Cruikshank's *Poor Bull & His Burden – Or the Political Murraion!* (*111*) shows John Bull collapsing under a huge burden of bishops, ministers, officers, tax collectors, etc. A similar print appeared as late as 1827 (BMC 15363).

Although criticisms of government patronage and corruption continued well into the nineteenth century, it was the irregularities and abuses of the electoral system that had become the chief concern of reforming opinion as early as the 1780s. Critics of the governing elite became increasingly convinced that the principles of the constitution were being undermined not just because of the executive's influence over the legislature, but because a narrow landed elite controlled the representation in the House of Commons and hence destroyed the democratic element in the constitution. These critics pointed out that every aspect of the electoral system benefited the landed elite rather than the people at large. In most constituencies the franchise was restricted to men of property and therefore only a minority of the total population had the vote. In the mid-eighteenth century fewer than 300,000 men in England and Wales had the right to vote out of a population of about 6½ millions. By 1831 the number of voters had increased by perhaps twenty per cent, but the total population had more than doubled. The distribution of parliamentary seats made the composition of parliament even more unrepresentative of the population as a whole. Only a minority of M.P.s sat for constituencies with electorates as large as 1,000 voters, while a high proportion of M.P.s represented small boroughs with restricted electorates. In 1793 Thomas Oldfield claimed that a mere 11,075 voters in England and Wales elected a total of 257 M.P.s.[25] Many large county and borough constituencies, especially London, were grossly under-represented compared to the five south western counties where there were numerous small constituencies. Many of the growing towns of the north and midlands – including Birmingham, Manchester, Sheffield and Leeds – had no representatives in parliament at all. General elections were only held every seven years, but what rendered the right to vote even less of a privilege was the infrequency of electoral contests in many constituencies. Only a tiny minority of counties went to the polls in any general election, while some small boroughs never went to the polls at all in the late eighteenth or early nineteenth centuries. Even when small constituencies did go to the polls the practice of open voting allowed the propertied elite to bribe, intimidate or cajole the tiny electorates into voting as their superiors thought fit. Efforts of this kind to influence the electorate were expensive and made electioneering increasingly the preserve of the propertied elite. Since candidates needed substantial property qualifications even to stand for election and since M.P.s were unpaid and therefore needed to be economically independent, only rich men or the clients of very rich men could expect to enter the House of Commons. Thus, the elected element of the legislature represented only a narrow section of the population and not the interests of the nation as a whole. The middling and lower orders came increasingly to regard this as a political grievance.

The irregularities of the electoral system were fully explored in the radical press, but the political caricaturists only explored certain of these abuses and did not even do this extensively until just before the Reform Bill of 1832. The caricaturists were mainly interested in election contests in and around London. These were untypical since the electorates were large and contests were common. The prints were therefore concerned with the personalities of the contestants and the issues which they personified rather than the defects of the electoral system itself. A few prints however (for example, BMC 4226, 5708, 10372) did condemn the corrupt electoral practices of particular candidates. More significant were the few prints which explored more fully the relationship between patrons, candidates and electors. In *Candidates canvassing for Seats in Parliament* (*91*) two grotesquely ugly candidates seek the vote of a poor ratcatcher who rejects the approach because the candidates' bribes are not big enough. Rather similar, but more sophisticated and perhaps more despairing, is Robert Seymour's *A Pot-Walloper*. In this print (*128*) a ragged, disreputable tramp, who, as a potwalloper, is one of the rare unpropertied men with a vote, is approached by two candidates. One urges him to use his vote in order to return an independent parliament, but the tramp takes more notice of the other candidate who offers him a bribe. William Heath's *General Election* (BMC 16163) warns voters that candidates make extravagant promises before the election, but ignore the interests of the voters once elected. Two similar prints, *The Genius of Elections or John Bull's Resolution* (80) and *John Bull and the Genius of Corruption* (84), portray a monster of corruption endeavouring to influence the votes of John Bull, but without success. Far less optimistic is William Heath's *How to get made an M.P.!!!* (129). This shows that voters, whether farmers or artisans, are utterly under the control of the patron of the constituency who is free to sell them to the candidate who offers the most. Should the voters resist the instructions of their patrons then the penalty could be severe. In George Cruikshank's *Freedom & Purity of Election!!!* (116) and in John Doyle's *Newcastle versus Newark* (126) the borough patrons of Tregony and Newark respectively are shown evicting tenants who have refused to vote as they were ordered. Much the most comprehensive indictment of the electoral system, however, is George Cruikshank's *The 'System' that 'Works so Well'!! – Or the Boroughmongers grinding machine* (136). This portrays the House of Commons as a decayed mill, whose water wheel is labelled with the names of rotten boroughs and from whose spout pours forth a stream of pensions, places, contracts, etc.

The caricaturists found it difficult to analyse the deficiencies of the electoral system, but they were in their element when faced with the task of attacking the arbitrary behaviour of those in positions of authority. Just as the political print was well suited to personalising the threat posed by leading radicals so it was an appropriate weapon for castigating the abuses of over-mighty ministers. Although a great many political prints produced in the late eighteenth and early nineteenth centuries were anti-radical, there were also a great many during this same period which were anti-ministerial. Indeed, several of the leading caricaturists were capable of producing prints of both types.

The threat posed to the liberty of the subject by royal ambition and ministerial tyranny was probably depicted more vividly and more effectively in political caricatures than in any other medium used by the critics of the constitution. From the beginning of George III's reign the caricaturists saw the Earl of Bute as the architect of a conspiracy to increase the King's power and to unbalance the constitution. Over four hundred caricatures – much the best evidence for the crescendo of abuse against him – attacked Bute. There was scarcely any line of criticism against him that was not portrayed in the prints. Bute regularly appeared as the overmighty subject possessing the instruments of corruption and disseminating places, pensions and bribes to the most degenerate of clients. In one print (10) Bute is Samson destroying the temple of the constitution and removing the supporting pillars of Magna Carta and the Glorious Revolution. In *The Vision or M–n–st–l Monster; address'd to the Friends of Old England* (4) he is a hideous dragon devouring Britannia and trampling upon the laws of England. In many other prints he is the minister behind the throne, or even literally behind the curtain, manipulating politicians. Long after he had lost all political influence he was still used by caricaturists to warn of a conspiracy against liberty.[26]

The fear that the Court was planning to undermine the constitution and subvert the liberties of the subject was encouraged by ministerial actions against John Wilkes and the American colonies in the 1760s and 1770s. The ministry's use of general warrants in order to arrest Wilkes, one of its most effective critics, was rightly regarded as an infringement of civil liberty. The successful efforts to exclude Wilkes from the House of Commons, after he had been duly elected on four occasions in 1768–9, threatened to undermine the right of the electorate to choose its own representatives. Wilkes was able to exploit these abuses of authority in order to raise widespread opposition to the aristocratic oligarchy which maintained a stranglehold on the political system. Recognising the value of publicity Wilkes exploited every available medium in order to reach as large an audience as possible. The caricaturists both served him and made use of him. Almost every incident of the Wilkes saga is illustrated in the political prints. Indeed, the context of popular emotion over the Wilkes affair is conveyed better in the caricatures than anywhere else. Many prints portrayed Wilkes as the champion of liberty engaged in a struggle against corruption and tyranny. In *The Many Headed Monster of Sumatra* (13) Wilkes fights the dragon of arbitrary power, a beast whose heads include those of Bute, Mansfield and Sir Fletcher Norton. In *The Colossus of the North* (23) Wilkes attempts to stem the tide of corruption which threatens to engulf parliament during the administration of Lord North.

The supporters of Wilkes were convinced that the treatment of the American colonies provided further evidence of a ministerial design to undermine the constitution. Several political prints explicitly linked the Wilkite and the American causes. The prints on the American crisis were almost entirely anti-Ministerial and were mainly pro-American. The caricaturists however found it difficult to do justice to the claims and principles of the American colonists. They saw the issue largely in British terms as a government attack on the liberty of the subject. It was the repressive measures of the government rather than the demands of the Americans that excited their interest.[27] In *The State of the Nation An. Dom. 1765* (8) Britannia attempts to console an angry and frightened America (portrayed as an Indian), who is being threatened by the naked sword of Grenville and defended by the Elder Pitt. In *The Able Doctor, or America Swallowing the Bitter Draught* (21) America (this time a female) is held down by Lord Mansfield and Lord Sandwich, while Lord North attempts to pour tea down her throat. The same ministers are shown operating a blacksmith's shop in *The State Blacksmiths forging Fetters for the Americans* (25), while in *The Closet* (BMC 5470) several ministers urge George III to be ruthless in his suppression of the American rebels.

In the 1780s and 1790s it was the Younger Pitt who became the ministerial symbol of oppression in numerous caricatures. Several prints (including BMC 6914, 8664 and 9038) show the ordinary subject collapsing under the weight of taxes imposed by Pitt's administration. Many more prints accuse Pitt of excessive political ambitions and of plotting to overthrow the constitution. In one print (37) he is at an altar sacrificing liberty, parliament, free elections, and the free press; in another (39) he is a vulture controlling the crown, gorging the Treasury and destroying Magna Carta; and in yet another (68) he is a skeleton breaking the pillars of the constitution and bringing down the benefits of trial by jury, Habeas Corpus and free speech. In probably the most all-embracing critique and the most effective satire of all, *The Dissolution; Or – The Alchemist producing an Aetherial Representation* (66), James Gillray portrays Pitt sitting on a military barracks before a furnace on which the House of Commons is dissolving in a glass retort. Magna Carta, the Bill of Rights, etc. are all collapsing. Pitt uses a bellows formed by a royal crown and beside him is a scuttle of 'Treasury Cole' heaped with guineas. In the vapour from the glass retort a new House of Commons is already forming with Pitt on a throne inscribed 'Perpetual Dictator' and M.P.s prostrating themselves before him.

It was not so easy to sustain the myth of a Court-inspired conspiracy against the constitution in the early nineteenth century. George III became increasingly popular as the figurehead of the coalition against Napoleon, while ill health rendered him politically ineffective. No royal favourite ever again matched the influence, or rather the supposed influence, of the Earl of Bute, no minister produced disaster on the scale of Lord North, and no Prime Minister dominated the political stage to the extent that the Younger Pitt had done. Nonetheless, there were occasions when the monarch or his ministers came under attack from the radicals and from the caricaturists for their arbitrary proceedings or reactionary policies. There were many prints condemning the heavy burden of taxation, expecially the income tax and, after 1815, the Corn Laws which were attacked for putting up the price of bread (see, for example, BMC 12503–7). The repressive measures of the government, particularly in the years from 1815 to 1820, produced some classic prints. In George Cruikshank's *Liberty Suspended! With the bulwark of the Constitution* (100) three of the most reactionary ministers – Castlereagh, Eldon and Ellenborough, sit astride a dismantled printing press. They reveal to a crowd of sinecurists and pensioners the hanging body of Liberty which is clutching Magna Carta, the Bill of Rights and Habeas Corpus and which is gagged with the government's recent 'Gagging Bill'. In 1819 there were several protests against the repressive nature of the Six Acts. George Cruikshank, although also critical of radical reformers, produced the most effective caricatures. In *Poor John Bull – The Free Born Englishman – Deprived of his Seven Senses by the Six New Acts* (112) Cruikshank portrayed John Bull as shackled, padlocked and gagged. Magna Carta and the Bill of Rights are pierced by a bloody dagger, while Castlereagh is depicted as a bird of prey. More popular and even more effective was Cruikshank's more subtle satire, *The Man in the Moon* (113). This caricature implied that the Six Acts could not in fact succeed in silencing the demands for reform. The Regent, on the moon, tries in vain to obscure the sun with a blanket on his sword. At the same time a comet rushes towards him, its head a cap of liberty and its tail bearing the word 'reform'.

The passing of the Six Acts did not stimulate as much indignation or as many political prints as did the violent attack on the radicals in Manchester in 1819 or the decision to put Queen Caroline on trial in 1820. The tide of opinion in the political prints was against the radicals in the years after 1815 until these two events reversed it.

Typical of the reaction to Peterloo was *Massacre at St. Peter's or 'Britons Strike Home'* (107) which depicted the soldiers in Manchester as the ruthless and deliberate assassins of women and children. George IV's decision to destroy his wife's reputation in order to prevent her being crowned in 1820 produced an astonishing flood of prints. The crisis was one of opinion and caricatures were exploited ruthlessly as anti-ministerial propaganda. They were – at least at first – the most effective contribution to the campaign against the King and his ministers. The prints were overwhelmingly in favour of the Queen and they did much to stimulate the radical onslaught on the government. After this campaign, however, the political prints never again launched an attack on this scale against the arbitrary proceedings or unconstitutional actions of the executive. During the crisis of 1830–2 the Duke of Wellington was caricatured as a militarist and as an overmighty subject, but he was not hated in the way that Bute or even Castlereagh had been.

3. THE REFORM OF THE CONSTITUTION

The political prints were overwhelmingly concerned with events at Court, in parliament, and in the metropolis. They underestimated the political significance of public opinion in the provinces, particularly in the new urban centres of the early nineteenth century. While they are an excellent guide to those political issues which aroused intense interest in the capital, they are a less satisfactory indicator of the strength of organised opinion in the country at large. The caricaturists were undoubtedly at their most effective when dealing with personalities and major crises and when attacking extreme radicalism or manifest abuses of authority. They found it difficult to explain abstract concepts or to subject political programmes to close scrutiny. The political prints are therefore a fascinating, but an uncertain, guide to the movement for constitutional reform which began with John Wilkes and culminated in the Reform Bill of 1832.

The political caricaturists were fascinated by the exploits of John Wilkes and by his success at personalising the cause of liberty. They never really explained however how his supporters elevated 'Wilkes and Liberty' into a major constitutional debate and organised support for Wilkes through a nationwide petitioning movement. There is not a single print illustrating the activities of the Constitutional Society or the Society for the Supporters of the Bill of Rights. One print, *The Conference* (BMC 4269), does allude to the 'instructions' which the Wilkite radicals proffered to parliamentary candidates in an effort to bind them to support the Wilkite cause should they be elected. Several prints, especially *The Petition of the Freeholders of Middlesex* (15) and *The Triumverate or Britania in Distress* (16), do show Wilkite petitions being presented, but they do not indicate the scale of the petitioning movement, its success across the country, or the means by which it was mobilised.

The American influence on the reform movement is fully recognised in the pamphlet literature of the 1770s and 1780s, but it is largely ignored by the political caricaturists.

The prints show no appreciation of the way in which the Americans extended English constitutional principles in a more radical direction and they betray little recognition of how American arguments changed the nature of reformist demands within Britain. The activities of the metropolitan radicals and the introduction of parliamentary reform bills in the House of Commons in 1783 and 1785 were entirely ignored by the caricaturists. The only possible exception is an uninspired and noncommittal print of 1788 which drew John Sawbridge presenting one of his regular motions for the reform of the system of representation (38). The caricaturists did seize upon one of the major demands of the Association Movement which sprang up in 1779–80. This was the demand for economical reform, that is, for a reduction in crown patronage and in the Court's corrupt influence over the legislature. The success of Dunning's famous parliamentary motion of 1780, that 'the power of the crown has increased, is increasing and ought to be diminished', was acclaimed in *Prerogative's Defeat or Liberty's Triumph* (28). A few prints did indicate general approval of the petitions of the Association Movement, but they did not explain the full extent of the reform proposals. The best of these prints – *Association or Public Virtue Displayed in a Contrasted View* (26) – is a complicated allegorical design in which the ghost of the Elder Pitt demands, 'O Cleanse yon Augean stables', pointing to the House of Commons which is 'Ruled by Powerful Influence'.

The political prints quite clearly reveal the intense emotions aroused in the 1790s by the revolutionary events in France, but they do not do full justice to the effect which these had upon both the demands and the organisations of the British reformers. Nearly all the caricatures on the leading radical propagandists, especially Paine, Price and Priestley, are extremely hostile. There are small portraits of the leading radical delegates arrested at the British Convention in Edinburgh in 1794 (BMC 8506–12), but these do not indicate either obvious approval or definite disapproval of their actions. An exception is a small engraving of Thomas Muir (54) that adds the caption 'Illustrious Martyr in the glorious cause/ Of truth, of freedom, and of equal laws'. As we have already noted the half dozen or so caricatures on radical organisations of the 1790s were all critical. So too is the print, *Copenhagen House* (62), which depicts a mass meeting of supporters of the London Corresponding Society in Copenhagen Fields in 1795. This mass rally of the brutish lower orders was addressed by John Thelwall and two other radical spokesmen. James Gillray did produce one print which contrasted French and British slavery (BMC 7546), though most caricaturists made the comparison in Britain's favour. Gillray was also prepared to endorse economical reform in such prints as *The Tree of Corruption – with John Bull hard at work* (67), in which John Bull tried to end sinecures, pensions and secret service expenditure, but he did not favour radical plans for parliamentary reform. One of the rare prints which was produced by the radicals themselves must have been counterproductive since it could only have confirmed the worst fears of the forces of order. *A Cure for National Grievances* (55), which was subsidised by a radical group, shows a crowd of pigs – 'the swinish multitude' – guillotining a crowned ass and threatening to do the same to the

Younger Pitt and John Reeves. The only print that puts a favourable interpretation on the radical campaign for parliamentary reform is an untitled caricature which may have been a frontispiece for a pamphlet. This print (76) shows Liberty under a tree which is nourished by radical works and which produces such fruit as religious liberty and universal suffrage.

It is only recently that historians have insisted that radicalism did not go underground for a decade after the conservative reaction of the late 1790s. Modern historians stress that radical activity soon revived, especially in the metropolis. The work of the caricaturists in fact confirms this interpretation. By 1802 Sir Francis Burdett and his supporters in Middlesex were attracting the notice of the caricaturists. Over the next decade and more Burdett appeared in a great many prints. Of even greater interest is the number of favourable prints on Burdett. Whereas the radicals of the 1790s were invariably condemned as dangerous fanatics, Burdett was seen by many caricaturists as the champion of liberty and as the honest opponent of ministerial corruption. Burdett was depicted attacking a giant red book listing the pensions and sinecures awarded in 1810 (87); portrayed as a knight in armour attacking a seven-headed monster of Treasury corruption (88); and praised as a Samson pushing down the pillars of corrupt representation and unlawful privilege (89).

After 1815 support for political reform spread from the small body of metropolitan radicals to the middle and working classes of the growing industrial towns. The widespread distress, which was caused by the post-war depression, the economic strains of rapid industrialisation and the bad social conditions of the new industrial towns, was the most important stimulus to renewed demands for parliamentary reform. The demands of the urban middle classes and especially the protests of the industrial working classes made political reform a major subject of debate in and out of parliament. The caricaturists, based in the City of London and in Westminster, did very little to dramatise in visual form the economic and social consequences of industrialisation. There is almost nothing in the prints to show the growth of industry, the conditions in the new factory towns, the development of trade unions and friendly societies, or the industrial disorder associated with violent strikes. Indirectly, however, the caricaturists did begin to reflect the social transformation of Britain. As we have already noted the increased production of prints, the professionalisation of the craft, and the growing proportion of prints with urban themes were all responses to the developing market for prints among the urban middle classes. The caricaturists also showed a greater awareness of working-class distress. This was reflected in their renewed attacks on royal extravagance, on the over-large civil and military establishments, on heavy taxation, and on the Corn Laws (e.g. BMC 12503–5, 12507, 12863). On the other hand, there were very few prints which took a favourable attitude towards the radical propagandists and their organised supporters. Henry Hunt and William Cobbett, in particular, were subject to much abuse in the prints. One of the very rare prints betraying any sympathy for the radical leadership was Robert Cruikshank's *Henry Hunt Esqr.* (95), which shows Hunt holding the Petition of Right and arguing in favour of moral pressure rather than physical force as the means of achieving reform. Most prints commenting upon the Cato Street conspirators of 1820 were fiercely hostile to this gang of violent revolutionaries, but one print, (*117*), did take the opportunity to condemn the government's use of agents provocateurs and another (BMC 13723) added to the execution scene of the conspirators the caption, 'The Radicals turned Traitors, . . . The guilty victims of a guilty age'. A more favourable attitude to the actual proposals for reform can be detected in a few prints. In *Blessings of Britain – Or – Swarm of Tax Gatherers* (96) John Bull defies a swarm of tax-gatherers with a pitchfork inscribed 'Prop of Reform'. More committed still was George Cruikshank's *Freedom & Purity of Election* (116) to which reference has already been made. This attack on borough patrons for evicting tenants who would not vote as they were ordered was inscribed with the words, 'Showing the Necessity of Reform in the Close Boroughs'. None of the caricaturists, however, took any notice of such radical organisations as the Hampden Clubs or the Union Societies. One very interesting and unusual print, *A Peep into the City of London Tavern* (101), did portray a meeting between Owenite supporters of villages of unity and co-operation and political radicals who insisted that distress could only be cured by political reform.

After 1820 the reform movement withered, largely as a result of improved economic conditions, but the caricaturists exaggerate the collapse of support for parliamentary reform in the 1820s. The Whigs brought several reform measures before the House of Commons during this decade, but none of them was noted by the caricaturists. Reform, even corruption, were almost forgotten by the caricaturists in the mid-1820s. On the other hand, when the debate on the old constitution intensified in the late 1820s and reached a crescendo in the early 1830s, the prints explored almost every aspect of it more thoroughly and more effectively than any previous political crisis.

The early signs of a revival of interest in reform were neglected by the caricaturists. The 'March of Mind' – the growing commitment to working-class education in the later 1820s – was treated with scepticism, even contempt, in the prints. The caricaturists were worried about too much education for the working classes, fearing that the labouring poor would neglect their daily work. The repeal of the Test and Corporation Acts in 1828, which was the first major alteration of the old constitution, was almost entirely ignored by the caricaturists. The one exception was William Heath's *Grand Battle of Lords Spiritual and Temporal or Political Courage brought to the Test* (122). This satire supported the alliance of Wellington and Grey against the reactionary forces led by Eldon. In 1829 the decision in favour of Roman Catholic Emancipation presented a much greater challenge to the Protestant constitution which had served the country so well since the late seventeenth century. Although the press, especially *The Times*, was largely in favour of this measure, most were hostile to any relief for the Catholics. In *The Battle of the Petitions, a Farce now performing with great applause at both Houses* (124) Eldon was now regarded as the heroic defender of the constitution against the combined onslaught of the forces led by Wellington, Brougham, Burdett and O'Connell.

The decline and eventual defeat of the Tories in 1828–30 marked, however, a profound shift in the political sympathies of the majority of prints. Criticisms of the Tories and support for parliamentary reform were now the dominant subjects of the prints. Wellington's towering prestige and his opposition to reform produced a large number of hostile prints which projected him as an authoritarian militarist and as an overmighty subject. As the economic situation worsened in the late 1820s Wellington and the Tories were accused of indifference to the distress which began to afflict large sections of the population. John Bull was once again seen to be ruined by the burden of taxation, as in *Poor Mr Bull in a Pretty Situation* (127), while the responsibility for the depressed state of industry and commerce was placed upon the financial exactions of church and state (125). The caricaturists did however transcend the old themes of ministerial corruption and John Bull's heavy tax burden. For the first time the prints explored the defects of the whole electoral system. We have already noted how some productions of the years 1829–31 condemned the undue influence which borough patrons could exert over the electors in the small rotten boroughs and how George Cruikshank offered a comprehensive indictment of the corrupt system of representation in his famous caricature, *The 'System' that 'Works so Well'* (136). Some prints offered positive suggestions for reform. One caricature (BMC 16289) actually endorsed the notion of voting by secret ballot, while another, *Which way would you prefer to get in* (143), favourably compared the large independent boroughs with the corrupt corporation boroughs and the rotten nomination boroughs.

The output of political prints reached its peak during the crisis over the Whig efforts to pass a Reform bill in the parliaments of 1831–2. The prints were overwhelmingly pro-reform although all political views were represented. The Whig case for reform was supported in such prints as *The Champions of Reform destroying the Monster of Corruption* (135) and *The Reformers' attack on the old rotten tree; or, the foul nests of the Cormorants in danger* (140), while the Tory hostility to reform was condemned in such caricatures as *Noble Lords opposing the Torrent of Reform* (142) and *Interior of the Tory Charnel House. Dissection of the Bill* (145). The main argument of those who opposed reform was, as before, that reform would inevitably lead to revolution and anarchy. In several prints (e.g. BMC 16815, 16991 and 17032) Earl Grey was shown to be in danger of falling into the abyss of revolution. In John Doyle's famous caricature, *Leap Frog, down Constitution Hill* (138), Grey and Henry Brougham leapfrog over the king whose crown is knocked from his head. Lord John Russell, who master-minded the Reform bills in the House of Commons, was accused, in *Little Johnny Rouse-Hell or the Ministers Last Shift* (139), of feeding Magna Carta, the Bill of Rights and other such guarantees of liberty to a monster of radical reform. In *The Cunning Men* (134) Grey and Althorp are magicians who have raised a devil which they cannot lay again. The demon wears a Jacobin cap of liberty with 'Reform' on its horns and 'Revolution' on its forehead. It breathes fire and smoke and cries out 'Vote by Ballot, Universal Suffrage, No Tythes, No Lords, No —'.

Although most prints support the moderate Whigs and their Reform Bill the fear of revolution was still so powerful among the caricaturists that they could very rarely bring themselves to support radical reform. The political riots of 1831, which put considerable pressure on the Whigs to continue with their efforts despite powerful Tory opposition in the House of Lords, were viewed with alarm by the caricaturists. The prints also revealed once again their relatively narrow social and geographic range. They largely ignored the activities of the powerful provincial political unions and of the organised working-class groups both in the capital and in the provinces. Two very interesting prints did at least indicate that the range of opinion on reform extended beyond the Whig and Tory positions. *Four Specimens of the Politick Publick* (*141*) recognised four main points of view: support for radical reform, support for the Whig bill, support for a more limited reform measure, and opposition to any reform. The second view was evidently regarded as the most sensible and responsible attitude to take. *Four Weighty Authorities on Reform* (*137*) shows four orators expressing these different viewpoints, but this caricature does not explicitly endorse the opinion of any of the orators.

The disputes on the Reform Bill produced a constitutional crisis because the Whig majority could ensure that the bill would pass through the House of Commons, but the Tory majority in the House of Lords could defeat the bill in that chamber. The attitude of the King, William IV, was therefore crucial to the success or failure of reform. Most caricaturists believed, wrongly in fact, that the King was an enthusiastic patron, almost the begetter of the bill. A few prints however recognised that William IV was not wholeheartedly committed to the cause of reform. In *A Fable for Ministers, the Grey, its Rider – & the Wild Fire* (*146*) the King is shown seeking the support of the House of Lords in order to avert the headlong plunge into revolution. In the *History of Canute* (*147*) William IV is encouraged by the Tories to resist 'the ocean of reform'. In the end, the King supported the Whigs and the bill passed through the Lords. The final passing of the Reform Bill was regarded as a great victory by many caricaturists. Robert Seymour's frontispiece to the poem *The Triumph of Reform* (*148*) shows John Bull kicking two M.P.s from rotten boroughs out of the doorway of the House of Commons. Many supporters of the bill had believed that, once passed, it would prove to be a cure for all manner of social and economic grievances which plagued the ordinary subject. This optimism is reflected in *The Stepping Stone or John Bull Peeping into Futurity* (*149*). Such high hopes were soon dashed. The poor in particular quickly realised that the Reform Bill had changed very little. In the *Present State of John Bull* (BMC 17202) the ordinary subject was shown to be still over-burdened with taxes and with very expensive civil and religious establishments. In *The Man Wot pays the Taxes!* (*150*) a ragged artisan protests, 'In what better condition am I now that the *Reform* Bill has past!' It was disillusionment of this kind that led to the rise of Chartism and to demands for a much more extensive reform of the constitution than had been achieved by the Great Reform Bill.

40

FOOTNOTES

1. These statistical details are based upon Charles Press, 'The Georgian Political Print and Democratic Institutions', *Comparative Studies in Society and History*, XIX (1977), pp. 216–38 and the British Museum *Catalogue of Political and Personal Satires* (hereafter referred to as BMC), eds. F. G. Stephens and M. D. George (11 vols., London, 1870–83, 1935–54).

2. M. Dorothy George, *English Political Caricature to 1792. A Study of Opinion and Propaganda* (Oxford, 1959), p. 131.

3. Ibid., p. 135.

4. John Brewer, *Party Ideology and Popular Politics at the Accession of George III* (Cambridge, 1976), p. 143.

5. John Wardroper, *The Caricatures of George Cruikshank* (London, 1977), p. 15.

6. BMC, X, p. 5.

7. Details from BMC, XI.

8. M. D. George, *English Political Caricature to 1792*, pp. 175–6 and BMC VII, p. 239.

9. BMC, VII, pp. 1, 3.

10. Ibid., X, pp. xii, xl–xliv.

11. M. D. George, 'Pictorial Propaganda, 1793–1815: Gillray and Canning', *History*, XXXI (1946), pp. 14–15.

12. M. D. George, 'America in English Satirical Prints', *William and Mary Quarterly*, 3rd series, X (1953), p. 518.

13. Draper Hill, *Mr Gillray, The Caricaturist* (London, 1965) p. 24.

14. Horace Twiss, *The Public and Private Life of Lord Eldon* (3 vols., London, 1844), I, p. 162.

15. M. D. George, *English Political Caricature to 1972*, p. 196.

16. Draper Hill, *Mr Gillray, The Caricaturist*, p. 54.

17. Ibid., p. 55.

18. M. D. George, *English Political Caricature 1793–1832. A Study of Opinion and Propaganda* (Oxford, 1959), pp. 35–6.

19. Draper Hill, op. cit., pp. 56–72 and M. D. George, 'Pictorial Propaganda, 1793–1815: Gillray and Canning', *History*, XXXI (1946), pp. 9–25.

20. BMC, X, pp. xiv, xvi.

21. John Wardroper, op. cit., pp. 15–18.

22. Charles Press, op. cit., pp. 223–6.

23. Details from BMC, V–XI.

24. H. T. Dickinson, *Liberty and Property. Political Ideology in Eighteenth-Century Britain* (London, 1977), chapter four.

25. Ibid., p. 238.

26. John Brewer, 'The Faces of Lord Bute: A Visual Contribution to Anglo-American Political Ideology', *Perspectives in American History*, VI (1972), pp. 95–116.

27. M. D. George, 'America in English Satirical Prints', *William and Mary Quarterly*, 3rd series, X (1953), pp. 511–37.

THE PLATES

These notes are prefaced with the relevant number in the *Catalogue of Political and Personal Satires Preserved in the Department of Prints and Drawings in the British Museum* (eds. F. G. Stephens and M. D. George) 11 vols. 1870–1954, which should be consulted for further information. This is followed by the date of publication and engraver, where known.

1. BMC 3772   c.1760

    A satire on corruption. The Lord Chancellor and (perhaps) the Chancellor of the Exchequer drink with the devil. They are surrounded by papers and bags which reveal their corrupt purposes.

IN PLACE. EN EMPLOI.

2. BMC 3857   May 1762

A party of ragged, dependent Scotsmen meet Bute and the Dowager Princess of Wales. One Scotsman cringes, others express satisfaction with their rewards.

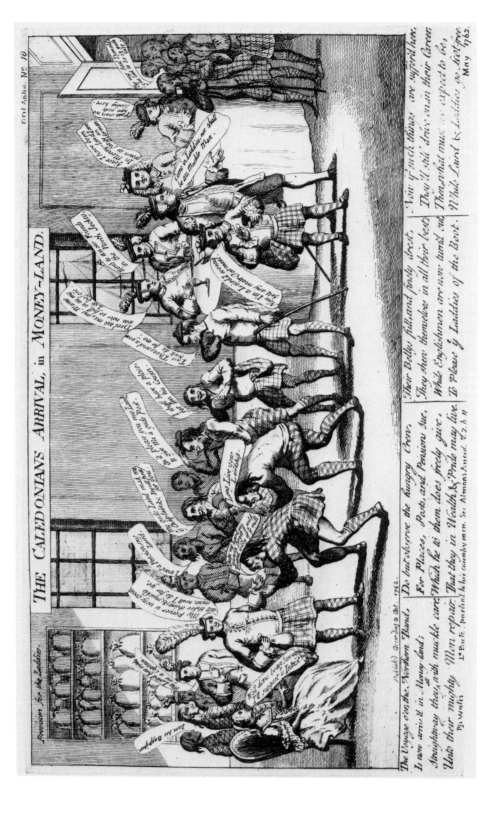

THE CALEDONIANS ARRIVAL, in MONEY-LAND.

3. BMC 3956   1762

John Wilkes, Charles Churchill, the Elder Pitt and the Duke of Cumberland fire arrows at a large jack boot (Bute) which has been set up as an idol. Arthur Murphy of *The Auditor*, Thomas Smollett of *The Briton*, and the Dowager Princess of Wales try to protect the boot. There are three Scotsmen in the distance and eight verses below the design.

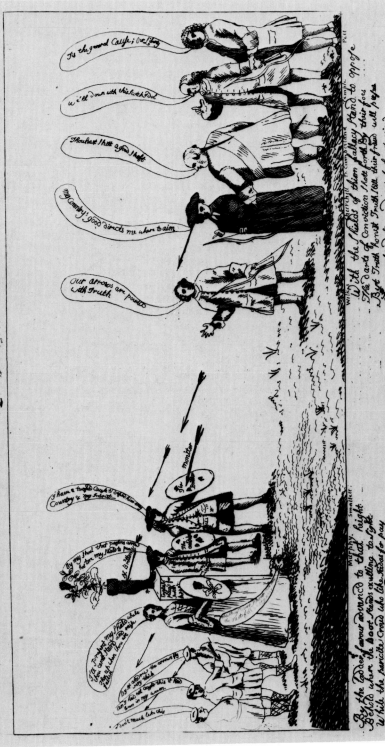

4. BMC 3983   1762
   Bute is shown as a hideous winged monster of tyranny destroying the liberties of
   the subject. The monster is aided by a goose (the Duke of Bedford) and a fox
   (Henry Fox). Two ragged Scotsmen drink from its teats. The man on the white
   horse referred to in one of the quotations is the Duke of Cumberland, Bute's
   opponent.

The VISION or M——l MONSTER;

addressed to the Friends of

Old England;

BY

Sybilla Prophecy.

These be thy Gods O Israel which
seek thy Ruin and bring Thee
into CAPTIVITY.

Vision Verified.

And I stood upon the
sand of the Sea, I saw a Beast
rise up out of the Sea, from the North
and many who were some of completion over
Shaped 5 Beast. Saying Who is like unto 5 Beast
And there was given unto the Beast a Mouth speaking
great things & Blasphemies & Power was given unto him
to continue at certain time, but caused all both small & great
rich & poor, free & bond to receive a Mark in their Right-hand
or in their Fore-head, and none might buy or sell save the Beast &
they who had received his Mark gathered together his
Honour & the Number of his Name, who so hath
understanding let Him count the Number of
the Beast for it is the Number of a Man &
his Number is 666 a certain Number
by the agreement of Heaven was crowned
of the Faithfull is always Twice over, and
stay — and Upon this Mark he'i poured out on the
from that mighty Rebel within,
Behold this!

Continued.

was with him, very fierce friends.
And I saw the Beast upon the White Beast
Going up he had like consuming ready to rise
and gentle Team fell upon the Beast and the
Beast and take it with him all that make had seen
and his Marks and worshipped. Him these with frightf
went above unto a Lake burning with Brimstone,
and yet detained into the word of heaven arose of
upon the White Horse and his armies Men and all
the fowls that fly in the midst of Heaven was filled
with their Flesh, and I heard a strong Voice
saying aloud, Honour and Glory be unto
Him that sitteth upon the White Horse
and may his Throne be exalted to
End of Time, & the Multitude of
AMEN.

Neither repent they of their Murder nor of
their Sorceries, nor of their fornication Theft save
not Mind to give their Power & Strength to 5 Beast.

L.d Bute

Sold —— by the Union Coffee-House in the Strand.

Bute re —— u —— 1 —— 6 —— 2

1763

5. BMC 4028   23 April 1763
   Wilkes, Churchill, William Pitt, and Earl Temple defend Britannia from the attacks of Bute and his Scottish allies. Wilkes has a 'North Briton' shield and stands over a prostrate Tobias Smollett, editor of *The Briton*.

WILKES, and LIBERTY.   A New Song.

To the Tune of, *Gee ho Dobbin.*

WHEN *Scottish* Oppreſſion rear'd up its d——n'd
  Head,
And *Old English* Liberty almoſt was dead ;
Brave WILKES, like a true *English* Member aroſe,
And thunder'd Defiance againſt *England's* Foes,
  O *ſweet* Liberty ! WILKES *and* Liberty !
  Old Engliſh Liberty, *O* !

With Truth on his Side, the great Friend of his Cauſe,
He wrote for the Good of his Country and Laws ;
No Penſion could buy him — no Title or Place,
Could tempt him his Country, or ſelf, to debate.
  O *ſweet* Liberty ! WILKES *and* Liberty !
  Old Engliſh Liberty, *O* !

To daunt him in vain with Confinement they try'd,
But ah his great Soul e'en the TOWER defy'd ; *30 April*
" *Conduct me, kind Sir* (to the Jailor he ſaid)
" *Where never Scotch Rebel, or Traitor, has laid.*"
  O *ſweet* Liberty ! WILKES *and* Liberty !
  Old Engliſh Liberty, *O* !

But the Jailor knew well it was not in his Power,
To find ſuch a Place any-where in the *Tower* ;
So begg'd, if he could, he'd the Lodging think well on,
Although it ſmelt ſtrongly of *Scotch* and *Rebellion.*
  O *brave* Liberty ! WILKES *and* Liberty !
  Old Engliſh Liberty, *O* !

The Friend of his Cauſe, noble TEMPLE appear'd,
(Brave TEMPLE, by each *English* Boſom rever'd) *30 April*
But ſuch was their Power — or rather their Spite,
That his Lordſhip of *Wilkes* could not gain the leaſt Sight
  O *poor* Liberty ! WILKES *and* Liberty !
  Old Engliſh Liberty, *O* !

One would think then by this, and indeed with ſome
  Reaſon,
That poor Colonel *Wilkes* had been guilty of Treaſon,
For ſure ſuch *good* People as now are in Power,
Would ne'er ſend an innocent Man to the *Tower.*
  O *poor* Liberty ! WILKES *and* Liberty !
  Old Engliſh Liberty, *O* !

To *Westminster* then they the Traitor convey'd, *May 3.*
The Traitor ! What Traitor ? Why *Wilkes,* as they ſaid,
But when he came there they were all in a Pother,
And they look'd, like a Parcel of Fools, at each other.
  O *poor* Liberty ! WILKES *and* Liberty ?
  Old Engliſh Liberty, *O* !

Then back to the *Tower* they whirl'd him along, *May 3*
Midſt the ſhouts and applauſe of a well-judging Throng
While the Dupes of Oppreſſion debated, I trow, Sir,
Moſt wiſely in private on what they ſhould do, Sir,
  O *poor* Liberty ! WILKES *and* Liberty !
  Old Engliſh Liberty, *O* !

Three Days had elaps'd when to *Westminster-Hall,*
They brought him again, midſt the Plaudits of all ;
When *Wisdom* and PRATT ſoon decided the Caſe, *May 6*
And *Wilkes* was diſcharg'd without Guilt or Diſgrace.
  O *brave* Liberty ! WILKES *and* Liberty !
  Old Engliſh Liberty, *O* !

Triumphant they bore him along through the Crowd,
From true *English* Voices Joy eccho'd aloud :
A Fig then for *Sawney,* his Malice is vain,
We have *Wilkes* -- aye and *Wilkes* has his Freedom again
  O *brave* Liberty ! WILKES *and* Liberty !
  Old Engliſh Liberty, *O* !   *May.* 1763.

Sold by E. SUMPTER, Three Doors from *Shoe-Lane, Fleetstreet* : Where may be had, The *British Antidote* to
Caledonian Poison, 2 Vols. Price 6 s.

6. BMC 4050   16 May 1763   William Hogarth
The famous satire on the 'patriotism' of John Wilkes, who leers and squints and who holds what purports to be the staff and cap of liberty.

John Wilkes Esq.

Drawn from the Life and Etch'd in Aquafortis by Will.ᵐ Hogarth.

Publish'd according to Act of Parliament May 4 16. 1763.

Price 1 Shilling.

7. BMC 4066   15 November 1763   Corry

The Earl of Sandwich (nicknamed 'Jemmy Twitcher') and supporters drag Britannia along, while trampling on the British lion, Magna Carta, etc. Henry Fox, Lord Holland, encourages him, 'Twitch-her, Twitch-her, Jemmy Twitcher'.

THE EXECUTION.

Twitch her Twitch her
Twitch her Tommy Twitcher.

Ay Ay, I've betray'd my Freind & now
Yo for You but Damn the Minority

Base Apostate Impeach Blasphemy,
yet commit Parricide.

Blasphemy

Perjury.

for messengers, Pimps,
Informers, Scotch spies & the

Carry Jaw.t

Carper.in.town. Sculp. 1764.

All hail Britannia, injured Maid
by Worthies such as these betray'd
In various Arts unrivall'd each.
These shall Forswear, & that Impeach.

What has Britannia left to hope
When Graceless Twitcher pulls the rope?
When old Corruption holds the bridle
And Gold secures the venal tribe.

8. BMC 4130   1765
   Britannia attempts to console an angry and frightened Indian (i.e. America) who is threatened by George Grenville who had introduced the Stamp Act. William Pitt, the Elder, tries to restrain him. The Earl of Mansfield, egged on by Bute, attempts to stab Britannia, but is prevented by Pitt's ally, the Earl of Camden. The latter denounces general warrants, which had been used against Wilkes, thus linking the cause of America with that of Wilkes.

The STATE of the NATION An: Dom: 1765 &c

9. BMC 4140   18 March 1766   Benjamin Wilson

A burial scene which is an allegorical satire on the repeal of the Stamp Act. The funeral procession for Miss Ame Stamp is led by Dr William Scott, who wrote pro-ministerial essays as 'Anti-Sejanus'. He is followed by Wedderburn, Norton, George Grenville (who carries the coffin), Bute (as chief mourner), Bedford, Halifax, Sandwich and two bishops. The ships are named after leaders of the repeal. The port represents the commercial interests which had opposed the Stamp Act.

THE REPEAL.

10. BMC 4179   1767

Bute pulls down the pillars of the temple of the constitution. Liberty topples from the top of the temple. Several politicians (Pitt, Granby and Lord Hawke) and the King and Queen also topple. This print appeared in John Almon's *The Political Register*.

Hitherto......I have perform'd.
Not without Wonder?
Now......such other trial
I mean to shew you of my strength, yet greater,
As with amaze shall strike all who behold,
This utter'd, straining all his nerves he bow'd,
As with the force of winds and waters pent,
When Mountains tremble, those three massy Pillars
With horrible convulsion to and fro

He tugg'd, he shook, till down they came, & drew
The whole roof after them, with burst of thunder
Upon the heads of all who sat therein,
Lords, Counsellors, or Priests,
Their choice nobility, & flow'r, not only
Of this but each Philistine City round,
Met from all parts.
Samson with these immix'd, inevitably
Pull'd down the same destruction on himself.

Samson Agonistes.

11. BMC 4192   March 1768

Two engraved designs. The first part shows the destruction of the ancient temple of liberty by Bute and his allies. Inside the temple is a statue of Wilkes. Bute tramples on Magna Carta, aided by Bedford, Lord North and others. The second part shows the temple restored by Wilkes, who is assisted by Camden, Temple and Pitt. The columns are inscribed with the names of patriots past and present. Below the design are eight stanzas of verse.

THE RETURN OF LIBERTY.

1768

LIBERTY REVIVED.

Tenax propositi.

I.

WHEN BUTE and his Faction had ravag'd the Land,
  And Old *English* Liberty hardly could ftand,
Then WILKES, the TRUE CHAMPION of FREEDOM, arofe,
Determin'd to combat his Country's dread Foes.
  Derry Down, &c.

II.

Notwithftanding their Power, their Craft, and their Spite,
Their Turning and Winding to prove Wrong was Right,
For his Country's Good ftill refolv'd to proceed,
He defy'd the bare Bums that came wigging from *Tweed*.

III.

When they found him fo ftaunch in his Country's Caufe,
To each one explaining the Senfe of our Laws,
They rav'd, and they rag'd, and they made a great Pother,
And ftar'd, like *Jack Puddings*, each one at the other.

IV.

Strait a Party was formed by SAWNEY the *Scot* ;
By St. *Andrew* they fwore, that WILKES fhould go to pot ;
Yet, in fpite of their Malice and d——'d Combination,
He his Honour maintained to all their Vexation.

V.

D——N, M——N and K——L, the Scum of the Nation,
By Perjury, Fraud, and by Affaffination,
With a B——fh——p, a J——dge, fully bent on his Fall,
Got *England*'s Friend banifh'd for—nothing at all.

VI.

Britannia was fad when fhe heard of his Fate,
And LIBERTY groan'd at her wofull Eftate :
In vain did they groan, and in vain did they figh,
In vain was their Sorrow, for WILKES was not by.

VII.

At laft he's return'd to his own native Ifle,
And the Genius of *Britain* comes forth with a Smile :
FREEDOM lifts up her Head, crown'd with Laurels again ;
For WILKES, fhe is fure, will her Honour maintain.

VIII.

Ye Livery of *London*, mind what you're about ;
Think who fhould be in, and who fhould be out :
On your Choice now your City, your Charter depend ;
And WILKES is the Man will your Freedom defend.
  Derry Down, &c.

12. BMC 4226   December 1768

This print, which appeared in *The Oxford Magazine*, contrasts the independent supporters of the radical candidate, Sergeant Glynn, with the bribed supporters of Proctor, the Court candidate. The Middlesex freeholders, with John Horne Tooke, support Glynn.

An Election Entertainment at Brentford.

13. BMC 4231 1768

   Wilkes fights a many-headed dragon of arbitrary power. The heads of the beast
   are those of Bute, Mansfield, Lord Holland, Sir Fletcher Norton, etc. The devil
   encourages the monster. Coming to the aid of Wilkes are John Glynn, Horne
   Tooke, the Marquis of Granby, and Earl Temple.

THE many Headed MONSTER of SUMATRA, or LIBERTY'S EFFORTS against MINISTERIAL OPPRESSION, A VISION.

1768

14. BMC 4239   1768

This print appeared in John Almon's *Political Register*. Wilkes stands within a fence marked 'the pale of English liberty'. He faces his chief enemies, Bute, Mansfield, Sandwich and the Dowager Princess of Wales. The King is blindfolded behind Bute. The genius of Truth hovers over Wilkes.

Malice and Fortitude.

There is no terror in your threats;
For I am arm'd so strong in honesty,
That they pass by me, as the idle wind,
Which I respect not _____

Shakespeare.

15. BMC 4290   24 May 1769
     Sergeant John Glynn, a leading Wilkite radical, leads other gentlemen in
     presenting the Middlesex petition to George III. The petition is printed below
     the engraving in three columns of letterpress. Justice and Hope are on the sides
     of the design.

Publish'd May 4 31 1769 by J Bowen   Opposite y Hay Market Piccadilly

To the KING's Most Excellent Majesty. The HUMBLE PETITION of the FREEHOLDERS of the County of MIDDLESEX.

Most Gracious Sovereign.

WE, your Majesty's dutiful and loyal Subjects, the Freeholders of the County of Middlesex, beg Leave, with all affectionate Submission and Humility, to throw ourselves at your Royal Feet, and humbly to implore your paternal Attention to those Grievances, of which this County and the whole Nation complain, and those fearful Apprehensions, with which the whole British Empire is most justly alarmed.

With great Grief and Sorrow, we have long beheld the Endeavours of certain evil-minded Persons, who attempt to infuse into your Royal Mind, Notions and Opinions of the most dangerous and pernicious Tendency, and who promote and counsel such Measures as cannot fail to destroy that Harmony and Confidence, which should ever subsist between a just and virtuous Prince and a free and loyal People.

For this disaffected Purpose, they have introduced into every Part of the Administration of our happy, legal Constitution, a certain unlimited and indefinite discretionary Power; to prevent which is the sole Aim of all our Laws, and was the sole Cause of all those Disturbances and Revolutions, which formerly distracted this unhappy Country; for our Ancestors, by their own fatal Experience, well knew that, in a State where Discretion begins, Law, Liberty, and Safety end. Under the Pretence of this Discretion, or, as it was formerly and has been lately called—Law of State—we have seen

English Subjects, and even a Member of the British Legislature, arrested by Virtue of a General Warrant, issued by a Secretary of State, contrary to the Law of the Land—

Their Houses rifled and plundered, their Papers seized, and used as Evidence upon Trial—

Their Bodies committed to close Imprisonment—

The Habeas Corpus eluded—

Trial by Jury discountenanced, and the first Law Officer of the Crown publicly insinuating that Juries are not to be trusted—

Printers punished by the Ministry in the supreme Court without a Trial by their Equals, without any Trial at all—

The Remedy of the Law for false Imprisonment barred and defeated—

The Plaintiff and his Attorney, for their Appeal to the Law of the Land, punished by Expence and Imprisonment, and made by forced Engagements to desist from their legal Claim—

A Writing determined to be a Libel by a Court where it was not cognizable in the first Instance; contrary to Law, because all Appeal is thereby cut off, and inferior Courts and Juries influenced by such Pre-determination—

A Person condemned in the said Court as the Author of the supposed Libel unheard, without Defence or Trial—

Unjust Treatment of Petitions, by selecting only such Parts as might be wrested to criminate the Petitioner, and refusing to hear those which might procure him Redress—

The Thanks of one Branch of the Legislature proposed

by a Minister to be given to an acknowledged Offender for his Offence, with the declared Intention of screening him from Law—

Attachments wrested from their original Intent of removing Obstructions to the Proceedings of Law, to punish, by Sentence of arbitrary Fine and Imprisonment, without Trial or Appeal, supposed Offences committed out of Court—

Perpetual Imprisonment of an Englishman without Trial, Conviction or Sentence, by the same Mode of Attachment, wherein the same Person is at once Party, Accuser, Judge, and Jury—

Instead of the ancient and legal Civil Police, the Military introduced at every Opportunity, unnecessarily and unlawfully patrolling the Streets, to the Alarm and Terror of the Inhabitants—

The Lives of many of your Majesty's innocent Subjects destroyed by Military Execution—

Such Military Execution solemnly adjudged to be legal—

Murder abetted, encouraged, and rewarded—

The Civil Magistracy rendered contemptible by the Appointment of improper and incapable Persons—

The Civil Magistrates tampered with by Administration, and neglecting and refusing to discharge their Duty—

Mobs and Riots hired and raised by the Ministry, in order to justify and recommend their own illegal Proceedings, and to prejudice your Majesty's Mind by false Insinuations against the Loyalty of your Majesty's Subjects—

The Freedom of Election violated by corrupt and undue Influence, by unpunished Violence and Murder—

The just Verdicts of Juries, and the Opinion of the Judges, over-ruled by false Representations to your Majesty; and the Determinations of the Law set aside by new, unprecedented, and dangerous Means; thereby leaving the Guilty without Restraint, and the Injured without Redress, and the Lives of your Majesty's Subjects at the Mercy of every Ruffian protected by Administration—

Obsolete and vexatious Claims of the Crown set on Foot for Partial and Election Purposes—

Partial Attacks on the Liberty of the Press: The most daring and pernicious Libels against the Constitution, and against the Liberty of the Subject, being allowed to pass unnoticed, whilst the slightest Libel against a Minister is punished with the utmost Rigour—

Wicked Attempts to increase and establish a Standing Army, by endeavouring to vest in the Crown an unlimited Power over the Militia; which, should they succeed, must, sooner or later, subvert the Constitution, by augmenting the Power of Administration in Proportion to their Delinquency—

Repeated Endeavours to diminish the Importance of Members of Parliament individually, in order to render them more dependent on Administration collectively. Even Threats having been employed by Ministers to suppress the Freedom of Debate; and the Wrath of Parliament denounced against Measures authorised by the Law of the Land—

Resolutions of one Branch of the Legislature, set up as the Law of the Land, being a direct Usurpation of the Rights of the two other Branches, and therefore a manifest Infringement of the Constitution—

Public Money shamefully squandered and unaccounted for, and all Inquiry into the Cause of Arrears in the Civil List prevented by the Ministry—

Inquiry into a Pay-master's public Accounts stopped in the Exchequer, though the Sums unaccounted for by that Pay-master amount to above Forty Millions Sterling—

Public Loans perverted to private Ministerial Purposes—

Prostitution of public Honours and Rewards to Men who can neither plead public Virtue nor Services—

Irreligion and Immorality, so eminently discountenanced by your Majesty's Royal Example, encouraged by Administration both by Example and Precept.

The same Discretion has been extended by the same evil Counsellors to your Majesty's Dominions in America, and has produced to our suffering Fellow-Subjects in that Part of the World, Grievances and Apprehensions similar to those of which we complain at Home—

Most Gracious Sovereign,

SUCH are the Grievances and Apprehensions which have long discontented and disturbed the greatest and best Part of your Majesty's loyal Subjects. Unwilling, however, to interrupt your Royal Repose, though ready to lay down our Lives and Fortunes for your Majesty's Service, and for the Constitution as by Law established, we have waited patiently, expecting a Constitutional Remedy by the Means of our own Representatives : But our legal and free Choice having been repeatedly rejected, and the Right of Election, now finally taken from us by the unprecedented seating of a Candidate who was never chosen by the County, and who even to become a Candidate, was obliged fraudulently to vacate his Seat in Parliament, under the Pretence of an insignificant Place, invited thereto by the prior Declaration of a Minister, that whoever opposed our Choice, though with but four Votes, should be declared Member for the County. We see ourselves, by this last Act, deprived even of the Franchises of Englishmen, reduced to the most abject State of Slavery, and left without Hopes or Means of Redress, but from your Majesty or God.

Deign then, Most Gracious Sovereign, to listen to the Prayer of the most faithful of your Majesty's Subjects ; and to banish from your Royal Favour, Trust, and Confidence, for ever, those evil and pernicious Counsellors, who have endeavoured to alienate the Affection of your Majesty's most sincere and dutiful Subjects, and whose Suggestions tend to deprive your People of their dearest and most essential Rights, and who have traiterously dared to depart from the Spirit and Letter of those Laws which have secured the Crown of these Realms to the House of Brunswick, in which we make our most earnest Prayers to God, that it may continue untarnished to the latest Posterity.   (Copy) *Signed by* 1565 *Freeholders.*

16. BMC 4298   5 July 1769
America (represented as an Indian) kneels before the throne and over the Stamp Act. Britannia appears in chains before Grafton, Bute and George III. She holds papers protesting at corruption and ministerial oppression. Wilkes and his allies, the London liverymen, present a petition. The print is addressed to 'The Glorious Sons of Freedom, at the London Tavern, who nobly defended the Rights of their Country against an Arbitrary Administration'.

The TRIUMVERATE or BRITANIA in DISTRESS.

TO THE

Glorious SONS of FREEDOM, at the LONDON-TAVERN,

Who nobly defended the Rights of their Country againſt an Arbitrary Adminiſtration,

This PLATE is humbly INSCRIBED,

By their humble Servants,

EXPLANATION of the PLATE.

THE figures on the throne repreſent R-y-l-t-y impoſed upon, by G—n and B—e, G—n, by his taking the right hand of the ****, and B—e, by leaning on his ſhoulder, and taking hold of his ſc—r (which is here repreſented as an iron rod of correction) and whiſpering pernicious evils in his ear. The guards repreſent two Highlanders in the characters of Lictors, with their falces. Thoſe before the throne are America breaking the yoke of bondage, and trampling on the Stamp-Act; Britannia in chains mournfully ſuing, that the grievances of her ſons may be redreſſed, and herſelf ſet at liberty, but in vain. The lion is the emblem of England.

The proceſſion repreſents the Livery of London bringing their petition, and leading in Alderman WILKES in the character of Liberty. The figure in front is the Lord Mayor, the two on the right are two Aldermen, in the characters of Fortitude and Hope, the character of Fortitude ſupported by Alderman B—kf—d, that of Hope, by Alderman T—c—k. Next follow officers of my Lord Mayor, and the Livery. The figures ſupporting the City-Arms, the Stork and the Bale, repreſent the City and Commerce. The Armour, the Sword of Juſtice, the Bible, and Magna Charta, are thrown by as uſeleſs to Britannia.

The three medals repreſent Oliver Cromwell, Charles the Second, and James the Second.

The picture repreſents that part of the hiſtory of Henry the Third, where he meets with many mortifications from his parliament and people, who at length obliged him to renew the two Charters, which was done in Weſtminſter-hall in the following manner, viz. The Peers being aſſembled in the preſence of the King, each holding a lighted taper, the Archbiſhop of Canterbury denouncing a terrible curſe againſt thoſe who ſhould violate the laws, or alter the conſtitution of the kingdom; then the Charters were read aloud, and confirmed by the King, who, all the time, kept his hand on his breaſt: after which every one threw his taper on the ground to raiſe a great ſmoke, and wiſhed that thoſe who violated the Charters might ſmoke in Hell.

O Muſe inſpire me while I write
This ſubject, hateful to indite.
Not with malice, ſpite, or gall,
But with juſtice, due to all,
Nor ſtrain, nor let my ſubject fall.
View the late Guardian of our iſle,
Who drooping ſees, tho' wont to ſmile:
By G—lle—n ſhackled with oppreſſion,
Of mighty ills, a long ſucceſſion,
Woes upon woes, to our diſgrace,
E'er ſince this D—e of B—fl—d race
Our gracious K—g on high did place.
Our cauſe he left, to join with B—te,
Shifting the ſcene as it might ſuit,
His luſt of power, of fraud, deceit,
His King, his country, to cheat,
What elſe expect, when fiends agree,
To root out blooming Liberty;

And place fierce tyranny in it's ſtead?
The cauſe that loſt Firſt Charles his head,
And Second James to loſe his right,
And meanly ſave himſelf by flight,
To find refuge where reigns oppreſſion,
Rather than make a juſt conceſſion,
For inj'ries done unto this nation,
By a moſt vile Adm—n:
From which (pray God) our King defend,
And glory crown his latter end:
Couns'llors may he chuſe, whoſe ſole ends
To our own country's glory tends,
Equal to King and country, friends,
Inſtead of diſcord, envy, ſtrife,
Which marks his preſent ſtage of life.
Prerogative and priv'lege weigh,
In equal balance let them ſway,
When the K—g commands, we'll all obey.

But of theſe things, why need we fear?
Behold—ſtern America there,
Tho' doom'd to feel the mighty ſtroke,
The galling chain, the hateful yoke,
But with reſentment and diſdain,
Breaks the yoke, throws off the chain,
For free, ſhe ever will remain;
And boldly dares thus to be free,
And barter life for Liberty.
With manly ſtride and reverence due,
Their Virtue's plan to purſue;
Behold fam'd London City—
Hope, Fortitude, they lead the van,
The attributes of honeſt man,
With juſt endeavours to be free,
And join with glorious unity,
To reinſtate bright Liberty.

May curſes heavy on them wait,
Who dare defile our glorious ſtate.
No patch'd-up venal, mean addreſs,
Submiſſive ſlavery to expreſs,
But heart and hand conjoin;
True records, they manly bear,
Hoping to awake the Royal ear,
With truths ſincere—
Fame's trumpet ſounds to hail the King;
Let's join aloud his fame to ſing.
May God awake our Royal King,
That through the earth his fame may ring,
And call him Father, Patriot, Free,
To ſuch as honour's paths forego.
Then bleſſings ever good, and great,
Will on him, and his iſſue wait.

17. BMC 4315   21 December 1796

A man divided into two halves. One half is Bute supporting the principles of
arbitrary government, the other is Wilkes supporting the principles of liberty.

The Times
Taken from an Original Character which appeared at the Masquerade at Lincoln
Decr the 21st 1769

Price 1.6

18. BMC 4368   January 1770

Britannia, fainting, is presented with petitions against corrupt practices. She is surrounded by Grafton, Mansfield and Fletcher Norton, who support arbitrary power. Temple, Rockingham and Chatham, the leaders of the opposition in parliament, protest. This print appeared in *The Oxford Magazine*.

Britannia in Distress.

19. BMC 4430   1770

A triangle of three poles representing King, Lords and Commons. This supports a large balance. On one side are symbols of liberty, on the other is an empty scale which Bute is weighing down with the aid of the King's little finger. This print was published in *The London Museum*.

The Constitution.

The Justices were all for Law; and nothing would please them but
Law; but they should find that the King's Little Finger should
be heavier than the Loines of the Law.

Impeachment of Lord Strafford.
Article 2.

20. BMC 4436   1770
This was engraved for the *Freeholders Magazine*. Britannia, half stripped and wounded, is attacked by Bute as a devil with goat's legs. He is assisted by a fox (Lord Holland), an owl (Sir Fletcher Norton), a bear (Lord Mansfield), an ape (Grafton), a negro (Jeremiah Dyson) and a crocodile.

Engraved for the Freemasons Magazine.

Britannia's treatment from her sham Friends.

21. BMC 5226   1 May 1774
A female (representing America) is held down by Mansfield and Sandwich, while Lord North pours tea down her throat. Bute stands by with a drawn sword. Britannia covers her eyes, while France and Spain show interest and concern. There are references to the Boston petition and the Boston Port Bill. This print was published in the *London Magazine*.

Boston cannonaded.

Boston Port Bill.

Boston Petition.

Military Law.

The able Doctor; or America Swallowing the Bitter Draught.

22. BMC 5240   1774?

Three sturdy trunks (King, Lords and Commons) stand against one another in the form of a tripod. Equally balanced scales are in the centre. One supports religion, law and authority, the other liberty, right and obedience. It is an attempt to portray the merits of Britain's mixed government and balanced constitution.

23. BMC 5242   1 December 1774

Lord North strides across a stream which flows from Westminster Hall. He stands on two blocks – Tyranny and Venality – and holds three papers (Places, Pensions and Lottery tickets) in one hand and a flaming torch inscribed 'America' in the other. Floating down the stream are a number of M.P.s. Britannia protests at this wholesale corruption, while Wilkes attempts to stem the stream with a broom. This was published in the *London Magazine*.

The Colossus of the North :or: The Striding Boreas.

I'll Stem the Stream.

Those that Should have been my Defenders have been my Destroyers.

Places
Lottery Tickets Pensions
Reversions

See our Colossus Strides with Trophies crownd.
And Monsters in Corruption's Stream abound.

1774

24. BMC 5281   1 January 1775
Politicians sit around a table in the House of Commons. Lord North distributes bribes, while, on the wall, a map of North America is bursting into flames. Wilkes and John Glynn petition against the ministers. This print appeared in the *Westminster Magazine*.

North America

A Remonstrance against the Proceedings of the Min.rs of the Prince

Dec. 1774.

The Council of the
Rulers, & the Elders, against the Tribe of ÿ Americanites.

25. BMC 5328   1 March 1776
    Lord North, Mansfield, Bute and Sandwich operating a blacksmith's shop in
    which they are preparing chains for the American colonies. George III smiles
    through the window.

An Act for
Prohibiting
all Trade &

THE STATE BLACKSMITHS
Forging fetters for the Americans

Published according to Act of Parliament 1st March 1776.

26. BMC 5638   15 February 1780   James Sayers
This is several sections combined in one design. One part shows a procession of
men presenting petitions, led by the petition from York. A monster outside the
royal closet faces the petitioners. Another shows Lord North, Bute and a female
figure attacking the pedestal of Britannia who protests at ministerial
corruption. William Pitt, Earl of Chatham, remonstrates with them. A third
shows M.P.s in procession receiving bribes, while a man holds out a list of
grievances.

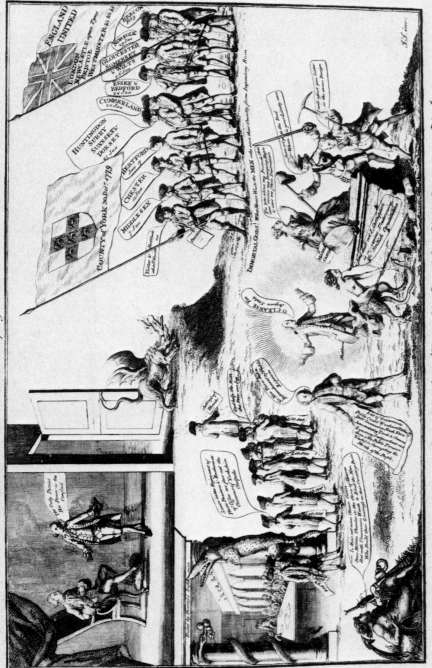

ASSOCIATION, or Public Virtue Displayed in a Contrasted View.

27. BMC 5657   6 April 1780
    Association Meeting at York
    The arms of the city of York are above the design. Christopher Wyvill chairs a
    meeting of reformers. Four female figures – Hope, Election, Public Virtue, and
    Liberty – approach. So do figures representing Commerce, Manufacture, the
    Landed Interest, and Public Credit. In the foreground is the British lion which is
    being unchained. A cock and a peacock, representing France and Spain, express
    disappointment, while Britannia and America embrace. The artist clearly hopes
    that the Yorkshire Association will produce peace and reform.

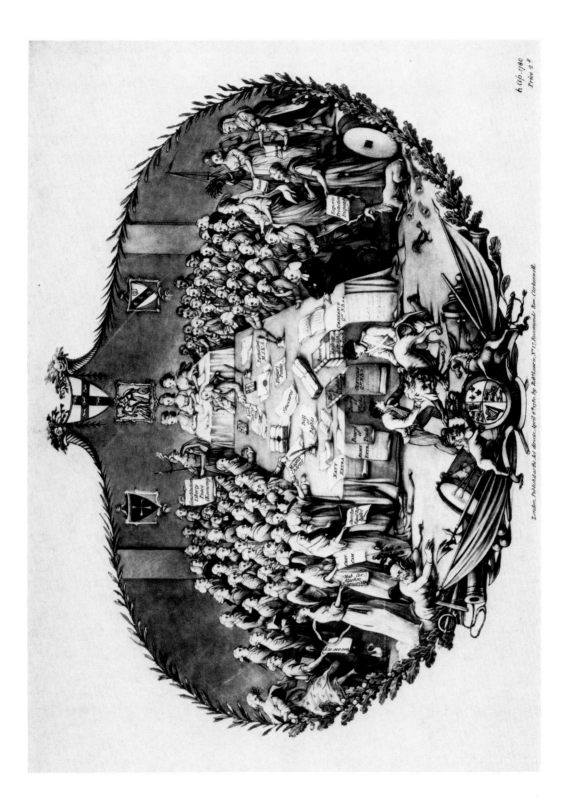

London, Publish'd as the Act directs, April 6.th 1780, by Ba[?]tolozzi, N.o 13, Rosomand's Row, Clerkenwell.

6 Ap. 1780
Price 2.s

28. BMC 5659   20 April 1780

A celebration of John Dunning's famous motion condemning the excessive influence of the crown. Dunning tramples on Lord North and Bute. He is assisted by Charles James Fox, but attacked by a Scot (obviously a supporter of Bute). Ireland and America express satisfaction at Dunning's success.

Ireland   America.   C.J.Fox   D. Bute.   Dunning   L.d North

PREROGATIVES DEFEAT or LIBERTIES TRIUMPH

29. BMC 5665   8 May 1780   Richard Sneer?
   This is a satirical attack on the petitioners of the Association Movement, who
   are regarded as poor republicans supporting rebellion not campaigners for
   liberty. The republicans are in poor dress and use an inverted crown and an
   inverted mitre as chamber pots. Below the design there is a short satirical verse.

A Petitioning. Remonstrating. Reforming. Republican.

Liberty
Rebellion

YOUR PETITIONER SHEWETH,

That he Humbly wishes to

Reduce y[e] Church to Gospel Order
By Rapine Sacrilige & Murther
To make Presbyty supream
& Kings themselves submit to him

& not content all this to do
He must have Wealth & Honor too
Or else with Blood & desolation
He'll tear it out of the Heart of the nation

8 May. 1780

Pub.d acc[.] to Act. May. 1780 by W Darly 39 Strand.

30. BMC 5675   4 June 1780

George III rides Britannia and stabs her with a spear. He is aided by dogs with the faces of Lords North, Mansfield, Thurlow, Germain, Sandwich, Hillsborough and other ministers. The dogs bark at Liberty. Petitioners mass before the temple of patriotism in order to protect the constitution. Opposite them is the House of Venality (the corrupted House of Commons). In the background Bute stands on a hill with his arm around the devil.

THE R—Y—L HUNT or the PETITIONERS Answer'd

31. BMC 6246 27 June 1783 William Dent
    At a meeting of the Society for Constitutional Information Dr Towers, Lord
    Surrey, Sam House eat at a table. All three are stout. The table is covered with
    papers inscribed Magna Carta, Bill of Rights, etc. A waiter enters the room. The
    implication of the satire is that the members are republicans who are devouring
    John Bull and the constitution.

THE *Constitutional Society*

Dedicated to all great Corporations

Search SURREY and all England over,
In each HOUSE Beef & Porter sure.

One TOWERS of strength, and best defend
The CONSTITUTION to defend.

Design'd by Carlton
1.st Surrey B.of Norfolk.

D.r Towers.

Pub.d by W. Dent N.º 2. Strand June 27.1783
Sam House

Executed by J.r Wrings
27 June 1783

32. BMC 6380   20 January 1784   James Sayers
Charles James Fox looks in the mirror and sees the reflection of Oliver Cromwell in armour. This attack on Fox's dangerous ambitions made a great impression. Sayers was hired by the Pittites to help defeat Fox in the Westminster election.

The Mirror of Patriotism.

C. J. FOX

33.	BMC 6444	11 March 1784	Thomas Rowlandson
This is a counterblast to the previous print. Charles James Fox, in armour, attacks a many-headed monster labelled Tyranny, Despotism, Oppression, Secret Influence, etc. He carries the sword of justice and shield of truth. He is supported by English soldiers and the Irish volunteers. Behind the hydra there are four men capering around the Standard of Sedition. They may perhaps represent Britain's foreign enemies.

THE CHAMPION OF THE PEOPLE.

34.	BMC 6914	11 January 1786	William Dent
John Bull, in a rage, is made up of the various taxes, duties and financial burdens imposed by the Younger Pitt's government.

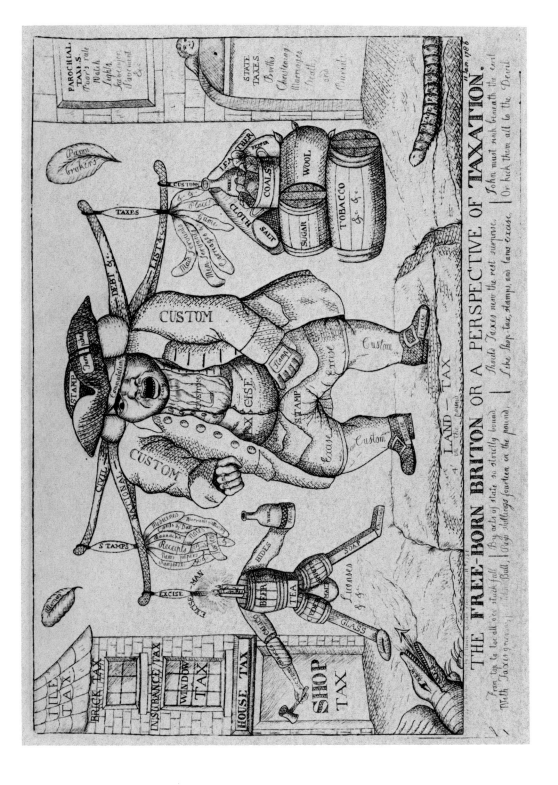

THE FREE-BORN BRITON OR A PERSPECTIVE OF TAXATION.

35. BMC 6945   21 April 1786   James Gillray
George III, the Queen and the Younger Pitt are at the Treasury distributing money and places to hordes of soldiers, placemen, etc. In contrast, an armless sailor and the Prince of Wales in rags are neglected. The Prince is offered a bribe by the Duke of Orleans.

TREASURY

Designed by Helagabalus.   A new way to pay the NATIONAL-DEBT, Dedicated to Monsr. Necker: Executed by Sejanus.

36. BMC 6962   28 June 1786   William Dent
    A snorting bull, representing the ordinary subject, is loaded with taxes. It lies
    down while Pitt, Henry Dundas and Richard Arden pull a load of loaves and
    fishes (corrupt rewards for placemen, etc.) from the bull's posterior.

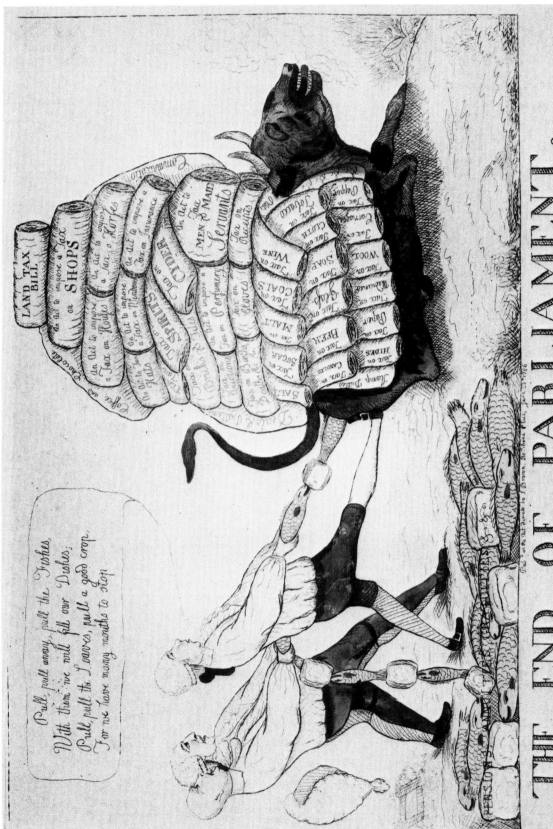

Pull, pull away, pull the Fishes,
With them we will fill our Dishes;
Pull, pull the Loaves, pull a good crop,
For we have many mouths to stop.

LAND TAX BILL

An Act to impose a Tax on SHOPS

An Act to impose a Tax on Horses

An Act to impose a Tax on Houses

An Act to impose a Tax on Windows

An Act to impose a Tax on Insurance

Commutation

Coffee

Chocolate

Tea

Tax on SPIRITS

Tax on CIDER

Tax on Perfumery

An Act to impose a Tax on Bricks & Tiles

Tax on Postilions

Tax on Gloves

Tax on Paper

MEN & MAID Servants

Tax on Receipts

Plate Glass

SALT

Tax on SUGAR

Tax on Candles

Stamp Duties

Tax on HIDES

Tax on BEER

Tax on Coffee

Tax on MALT

Tax on COALS

Tax on Soap

Tax on Leather

Tax on WINE

Tax on WOOL

Tax on Cloth

Tax on Cottons

Tax on Tobacco

Tax on Coffee

PENSIONS

THE END OF PARLIAMENT.

37. BMC 7124   8 January 1787
   William Pitt stands beside an altar burning books and papers representing the destruction of liberty, parliament, free elections, a free press, etc. Fox protests at the sacrifice and holds up a petition. 'Time' shows a picture of the future with Liberty dead and parliament ruined.

A Sacrifice to Slavery, dedicated without permission to the Puppet Players in Downing Street

38. BMC 7291   31 March 1788   James Sayers
John Sawbridge
John Sawbridge stands addressing the House of Commons, with a paper inscribed 'Motion for the Reform in the Representation'. Sawbridge repeatedly moved for leave to bring in reform bills, but without success.

Motion
for Reform
in the
Representation

Pub[lished] by J[a]s. Bretherton 31st March 1758

39. BMC 7478   3 January 1789   James Gillray
William Pitt is seen as a vulture grasping the crown and sceptre in one claw and the coronet of the Prince of Wales in the other. His breast is inscribed with the word 'treasury'. He is destroying Magna Carta. This is an attack on Pitt's role during the Regency crisis.

The VULTURE of the CONSTITUTION.

Pub: Jan.ʳ 3.ᵈ 1789. by H. Humphrey, New Bond S:ᵗ

40. BMC 7628   16 February 1790   James Sayers
     This is a satire on the efforts of radicals and Foxite Whigs to repeal the Test and
     Corporation Acts in 1790. Richard Price, Joseph Priestley and Theophilus
     Lindsey, who are all Dissenters, are in a pulpit. Price, in particular, is attacking
     the Church and the constitution and supporting the revolution in France. Fox,
     Stanhope, Thomas Paine and Andrew Kippis are in the congregation. Price's
     famous sermon to the Revolution Society, 'A Discourse on the Love of Our
     Country', led to his being attacked in Burke's *Reflections*.

The REPEAL
of the
TEST ACT a Vision

41. BMC 7630   22 February 1790   William Dent
This is another attack on the alliance of Foxite Whigs and radical Dissenters (including Joseph Towers, Price and Priestley) who are shown attacking a building inscribed 'Church and State'. They are charged with deism, republicanism, etc.

MEETING of DISSENTERS RELIGIOUS and POLITICAL 1790.

42. BMC 7636   22 March 1790   William Dent

Joseph Priestley preaches from a tub inscribed Fanaticism to Fox, the Prince of Wales, Townshend, etc. Priestley tells Fox that there is no devil, but the devil in fact crouches behind him.

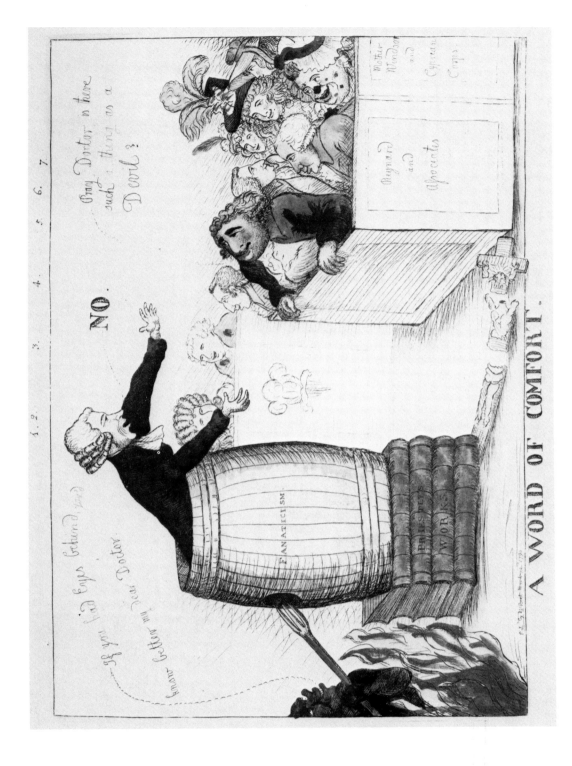

A WORD OF COMFORT.

43.   BMC 7822   1 January 1791   Samuel Collings?
Richard Price preaches from a tub inscribed 'political gunpowder'. There are several other slogans of a revolutionary nature. Price preached a famous radical sermon to the Revolution Society on 4 November 1790.

Tale of a Tub.
"*Every Man has his* PRICE!" *Sir R. Walpole.*

Published as the Act directs, by Bentley & C.º Jan.ʸ 1.ˢᵗ 1791.

44. BMC 7859   12 May 1791   James Sayers

This is a satire on the Society for Constitutional Information, the great disseminator of radical works. An ass, laden with radical books, brays 'Rights of Man' while kicking the British lion. An inscription prays, 'From all Seditions privy Conspiracy and Rebellion from all false Doctrine Heresy and Schism &c. Good Lord deliver us.' Adams was the Secretary of the S.C.I.

Right of Man
Paine

Reflections
on the
Revolution in
France
by the Right
Honble E Burke

Scarce
Pamphlets

Little Constitutions

Treasons

Moral Slang

Seditions Plots

Published by Order of the Society for Constitutional Information. By D. Almost Scott.

For all letters pay Conspiracy and Rebellion, from old fustic Doctor Terry... to great Lord Adam &c

The Gift is Solemn. Secretary to the Society for Constitutional Information. He is one & have received £50 down for allowing his name to be free to such seditious papers as any of the Members may spread by spying themselves.

45. BMC 7867   23 May 1791   James Gillray
Thomas Paine, grotesquely caricatured, measures a huge crown for a new pair of revolution breeches. This is a satire on his republicanism and his political ambitions.

Humbly dedicated to the Jacobine Clubs of France & England! by Common Sense
"These are your Gods, O, Israel!"

"Fathom & a half! Fathom & a half! Poor Tom!"
ah! mercy upon me! that's more by half than my poor Measure will ever
be able to reach! — Lord! Lord! I wish I had a bit of the Stay-tape or Buckram which
I used to Cabbage when I was prentice, to lengthen it out, — well, well, who could
ever have thought it, that I, who have served Seven Years as an Apprentice & afterwards
worked Four Years as a Journeyman to a Master Taylor, then followed the business of an
Exciseman as much longer, should not be able to take the dimensions of this Bauble? for what
is a Crown but a Bauble which we may see in the Tower for Six-pence a piece? — and, altho'
it may be too large for a Taylor to take Measure of, there's one Comfort, he may make mouths
at it & call it as many names as he pleases! — and yet, Lord, Lord, I should like to make it
a Yankee-doodle Night-Cap & Breeches, if it was not not so damn'd large or I had stuff enough
Ah! if I could once do that, I would soon stitch up the mouth of that Barnacled Empiric
from making of any more Reflections upon the Taints — So Silent & Liberty
for ever — & damn the Things

Pub.d May 28th 1791. by H.Humphrey
N.o 18. old Bond Street.

"THE RIGHTS OF MAN; — or TOMMY PAINE, the
little American Taylor, taking the Measure of the CROWN, for a new Pair of
Revolution-Breeches.

46. BMC 7890   12 July 1791   William Dent
Priestley, Fox, Towers and Sheridan all sing and dance around a cauldron which boils the crown, flag of liberty, etc. They are encouraged by demons. On the wall are four portraits of the reformers under the titles, 'Fanaticism, 'Wat Tyler', 'Republicanism' and 'Jack Cade' respectively. This is a satire on the planned dinner at the Crown and Anchor Tavern to celebrate the second anniversary of the fall of the Bastille.

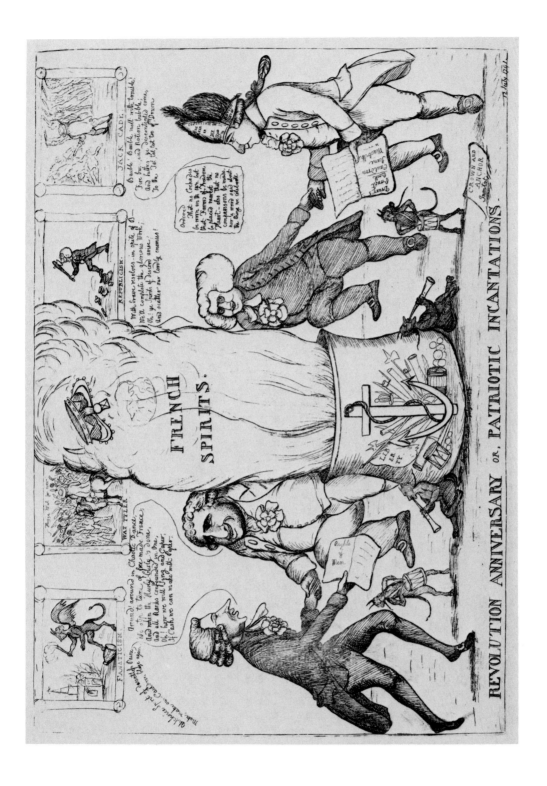

REVOLUTION ANNIVERSARY or, PATRIOTIC INCANTATIONS.

47. BMC 7900   1 September 1791   Samuel Collings?
An attack on Paine who is at his desk writing treasonable works.

MAD TOM.
or the MAN *of* RIGHTS

48. BMC 8087   14 May 1792   Isaac Cruikshank
This is an attack on Paine, Sheridan and Samuel Whitbread as conspirators and incendiaries. The Foxite Whigs did not in fact support Paine or his principles. In this print the three men are shown attempting to set fire to a building. An attempt was made to set fire to the House of Commons on 9 May 1792.

Mad Tom's first Practical Essay on the Rights of MAN

49. BMC 8131   15 November 1792   Isaac Cruikshank
Priestley and Paine sit at a table on which there are books on Fire, Murder, Assassination, etc. Pictures of assassinations and executions hang on the wall. The title refers to the Association of the Friends of the People, a Whiggish reform society.

The FRIENDS of the PEOPLE

50. BMC 8285   1 January 1793   Isaac Cruikshank
    A giant Edmund Burke, a dagger in each hand, in the House of Commons. He
    eats a scroll with the words 'Plunderers', 'Assassins', 'Republicans', 'Levellers',
    etc. on it. Charles James Fox flees. This is a satire on the famous melodramatic
    scene on 28 December 1792 when Burke produced a dagger, crying that this
    was what Britain could expect from France. He claimed that the dagger was one
    of many being manufactured in Birmingham for British radicals. This incident
    marked his public breach with Fox.

Reflctions on the French Revolution

51. BMC 8287   2 January 1793   James Gillray
A buxom Britannia is being forced into a very tight-fitting corset by Thomas
Paine, who was once a staymaker. Britannia has an expression of pained
reproach. Paine's face is blotchy and his expression fierce. A satire on altering a
good constitution to satisfy theoretical standards of perfection.

G.W: inv!

Pub.d Jan.y 2.d 1793. by H. Humphrey, N.o 18, Old-Bond Street

FASHION before EASE;

or, — A good Constitution sacrificed, for a Fantastick Form.

52. BMC 8291   15 January 1793   William Dent
Charles James Fox's body is laid bare as if for dissection. It is found to possess every possible personal and political failing. A similar dissection of Pitt can be found in BMC 9013.

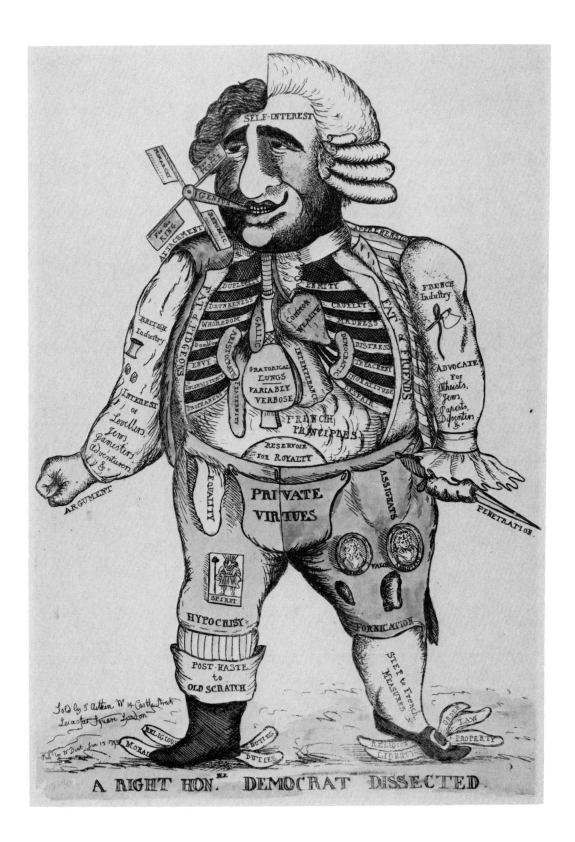

A RIGHT HON.ᴮᴸᴱ DEMOCRAT DISSECTED.

53. BMC 8320   8 April 1793   James Gillray
    William Pitt steers the ship of the constitution, containing Britannia, through a storm towards the haven of public happiness. He steers between the rock of democracy and the whirlpool of arbitrary power. Three sharks with human heads (those of Fox, Sheridan and Priestley) menace the boat.

SHARKS: _Dogs of Scylla._

BRITANNIA _between_ SCYLLA & CHARYBDIS.

or — _The Vessel of the Constitution steered clear of the Rock of Democracy, and the Whirlpool of Arbitrary-Power._

Pub.d. April 8.th 1793 by H. Humphrey N.o 18 Old Bond Street

J.Gd. the worship London publisher.

_Alto as steering Britannia, and the Constitution, toward the Shrine of Public Happiness between the Rock of Democracy,
and the Whirlpool of absolute Power, wille precisely represented by a juncture. Ruchick. On land. At Anche. Dogs of
Scylla, and Needless, Bequart Bourdeaux._

54.   BMC 8359   1793   John Kay
Thomas Muir
A small oval engraving of Thomas Muir, the Scottish radical, who was
sentenced to be transported because of his political views. One of the rare prints
which defended the radicals and regarded those who were punished as martyrs.
This has the inscription,
'Illustrious Martyr in the glorious cause
Of truth, of freedom, and of equal laws.'

I.Kay 1793

Illustrious Martyr in the glorious cause

Of truth, of freedom. and of equal laws.

55. BMC 8365   1793?
Pigs guillotine a crowned ass (George III) and threaten William Pitt and John Reeves. Burke had referred to the radicals as 'the swinish multitude' and some of them adopted the label with ironic pride. This print was subsidised by a radical group led by Citizen Lee at the British Tree of Liberty, 98 Berwick Street, Soho.

A CURE for NATIONAL GRIEVANCES.

REVOLUTION PLACE

THE KINGS EVIL, CURED GRATIS.

Dr Guillotine.

56. BMC 8424   9 January 1794   Isaac Cruikshank

The forces of good and evil converge on the temple of the British constitution which has the three pillars of King, Lords and Commons and Britannia underneath the dome. Fox and Sheridan, aided by the radicals of the London Corresponding Society, the British Convention, etc., threaten to blow up the temple. William Pitt leads the forces of order behind a solid barrier. The print is dedicated to John Reeves' loyalist organisation, the Association for the Preservation of Liberty and Property against Republicans and Levellers. There is a verse below the design.

A PICTURE OF GREAT BRITAIN IN THE YEAR 1793.

Publ. by I. Alexander, 373 Strand London
January 1. 1794

DEDICATED TO THE ASSOCIATIONS
for Preserving Liberty and Property
against Republicans and Levellers.

57.   BMC 8426   10 February 1794   Isaac Cruikshank
A group of English sansculottes, including Fox, Sheridan, Stanhope, Whitbread,
Bedford and Thomas Erskine, take offerings to a hideous woman who
represents republican liberty. The Foxite Whigs opposed the war with
revolutionary France.

The British Delegates Respectful application for Peace.

A PEACE OFFERING. To the Genius of LIBERTY and EQUALITY.
Dedicated to those Lovers of French Freedom who would thus Debase their Country

58. BMC 8617   1795   James Sayers
Four radical citizens of Norwich, sitting on a bull, kneel before a group of
Frenchmen with the heads of animals. This is a satire on the foolishness of the
British radicals who maintained contact with revolutionary France. Sayers
himself was from Yarmouth and was much opposed to the Norfolk radicals.

59. BMC 8624   2 March 1795   James Gillray
Fox, Stanhope, Sheridan and other English sansculottes take over the House of Commons by force and make William Pitt their prisoner. Radical books lie on the table, while Magna Carta and the Bible are being burned. The lower orders take over the seats in the House of Commons.

Pub.d March 4.t 1795. by H. Humphrey, N.o 37. New Bond Street.

Vide Cornwall &c.

Frederic's Patriotic Regeneration —viz.— Parliament Reform'd, à la Françoise.— that is,— Honest Men (i.e. Opposition) in the Seat of Justice.

60. BMC 8664   6 July 1795

William Pitt, much caricatured, rides John Bull and lashes him with war, taxes, monopoly, oppression, etc. In the background the London Corresponding Society holds a meeting. It actually held a meeting in St. George's Fields on 29 June 1795.

BILLYS HOBBY-HORSE or JOHN BULL Loaded with MISCHIEF.

61. BMC 8672   14 August 1795   Isaac Cruikshank
William Pitt is portrayed as a giant locust ruining the constitution and the country with his taxes and oppressive measures.

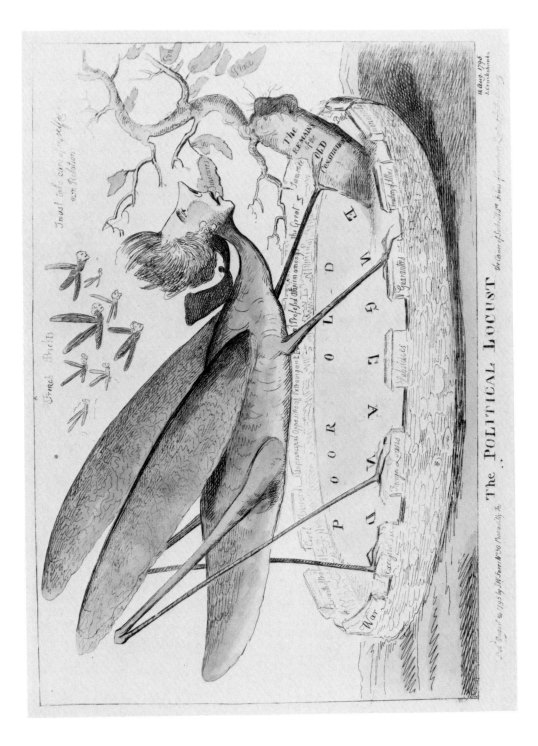

The POLITICAL LOCUST

62. BMC 8685   16 November 1795   James Gillray
A vast crowd of the lower orders, who are ragged and brutish, are addressed at a mass meeting called by the London Corresponding Society at Copenhagen Fields. Three platform speakers – John Thelwall, John Gale Jones and William Hodgson – address the crowd. The L.C.S. held mass meetings on 26 October and 12 November 1795.

COPENHAGEN HOUSE.

63. BMC 8687   17 November 1795   Benjamin West?
A huge William Pitt towers over a crouching John Bull who is burdened with taxes, pensions, subsidies, etc. Pitt holds a huge club labelled Convention Bill, which refers to two acts recently passed to suppress seditious meetings and treasonable practices.

Pensions
Subsidies
Tax
Taxation
Debt

Convention Bill

17 Nov. 1795
West

The MODERN HERCULES
a Finishing Blow for Poor John Bull

64. BMC 8701   1 December 1795   Isaac Cruikshank
William Pitt, as Gulliver, puts an extinguisher over a crowd of Lilliputian
radicals meeting in Copenhagen Fields. Among the radicals are Stanhope, Fox,
Sheridan and Thelwall. This is a satire on the Treasonable Practices and
Seditious Meetings Acts of 1795.

The ROYAL EXTINGUISHER or GULLIVER Putting out the PATRIOTS of LILLIPUT

65. BMC 8780   25 January 1796   George Woodward?
   This is another satire on the repressive nature of the Two Acts of 1795. Six
   elderly citizens, all of them muzzled, sit around a table. Wall posters proclaim
   that they cannot be allowed to think.

Rules to be observed
by
The Thinking Club.
Chairs to be taken at eight
To prevent any member from
Letting his tongue run
Constitutional muzzles
are sold at the door
That mum be the Order
of the day
The president to signify the
subject to be thought on in
writing in a conspicuous
Part of the room

Question to be thought on this Evening
How long may we be permitted to Think?

A THINKING CLUB.

Pub. Jan.ᵈ 25 1796 by S.ᵗ W.ᵐ N.ᵒ 8 Piccadilly corner of Sackville Street N.ᵒ Folios of Caracatures lent out for the Evening

66. BMC 8805   21 May 1796   James Gillray
William Pitt sits on a military barracks before a furnace on which the House of
Commons is dissolving in a glass retort. Magna Carta, the Bill of Rights, etc. are
all collapsing. Pitt uses a bellows formed by a royal crown and beside him is a
scuttle of 'Treasury Cole' heaped with guineas. In the vapour from the glass
retort a new House of Commons is already in being with Pitt on the throne
which is inscribed 'Perpetual Dictator' and M.P.s prostrating themselves before
him. This is an attack on the ambitions and oppressive policies of Pitt,
particularly on the dissolution of Parliament on 19 May and the decision to
build military barracks without parliamentary sanction.

The DISSOLUTION, _or_ The Alchymist producing an Æthirial Representation.

67. BMC 8817   22 June 1796   James Gillray

John Bull tugs on a rope around a tree in which there are the heads of Pitt, Henry Dundas and perhaps Loughborough and also three money bags labelled 'sinecures', 'pensions', 'secret service money', etc. John Horne Tooke urges the pulling down of the tree of corruption. A caption suggests that the tree can only be destroyed by laying an axe to the roots. There are quotations from speeches made at the Westminster election of 1796. Gillray has adopted a deliberately childish style in this print, perhaps to mask his attack on Pitt and his administration.

The TREE of CORRUPTION, — with John Bull hard at work.

"Yes, honest John! by your Pulling, you have Shaken it! — pull again Now it will Totter, — pull once more, & it will fall." Nota. Horne Tooke loquitur.

Answer to Horne Tooke { You may pluck up a Hazel, & pull up a Pea, | And so Honest John if you'd pluck off the Fruit,
{ But there ne'er was a Man, that could pull down a Tree. | Leave pulling alone, lay the Ax to the Root!

68. BMC 9002   1 April 1797
A skeleton William Pitt breaks the pillars of the constitution labelled 'Lords'
and 'Commons'. Falling blocks from the building are labelled 'Civil List', 'Trial
by Jury', 'Habeas Corpus', 'Freedom of Speech', etc. Britannia weeps, while
Liberty and Truth have been hanged. This is a sharp attack on Pitt's repressive
measures of this period. It is an old-fashioned emblematic print.

Ayex **PITiè de NOUS!!**

The Cloud capt Towers &
Pub^d as the Act directs April 1st 1797 by the Kings Friend

69. BMC 9018   28 May 1797   James Gillray

Fox, Charles Grey, Sheridan, Thomas Erskine and other Foxite Whigs – in the form of rats – flee from the Opposition benches of the House of Commons. The Speaker is astonished, while Pitt calmly addresses the house. After the failure of Charles Grey's motion for a reform of parliament in May 1797 the opposition temporarily seceded from the House of Commons, a move which was much criticised. Wallposters in the House proclaim, 'Virtue Triumphant or the Expulsion of Vice' and 'Opposition Silenced'. Dundas and Wilberforce sit next to Pitt.

PARLIAMENTARY REFORM, _or_ _Opposition Rats, leaving the House they had Undermined._

70. BMC 9055   c.1797

A caricature of a fierce and ragged Jacobin with a dagger, a model guillotine and a sheaf of papers referring to Paine's *Rights of Man*, assassinations, etc. 'Democrat' was often used as a term of abuse to mean a violent revolutionary.

Guillotine

Assassination

Paine's Rights of Man

Equality

London: Printed for Bowles & Carver.   No. 69 St. Paul's Church Yard

A DEMOCRAT.

Dighton del.

71. BMC 9178   28 February 1798
     A monstrous and hideous creature, representing the horrors of democracy, sits with Fox on one knee and Horne Tooke on the other. They are surrounded by an abyss.

The Hopes of the Party! or the Darling Children of Democracy!

72. BMC 9190   20 March 1798   James Gillray
John Bull kneels before a monstrous head of Fox which roars, 'Radical Reform – or Ruin! Destruction Debt! Misery!' etc. This is an attack on Fox's speech on reform during the debate on assessed taxes on 4 January 1798.

Many cries how he does roar it away. / I ne'er was in such a fright in all my born / days; this is worse than the afscha Taxes!!

Rascal Reform or Ruin Deduction / 1661 Whorely Party Slavery! Oppression Self of / Honesty Religion — think of your Religion. Jehovah!!

JOHN BULL, Consulting the ORACLE!

73. BMC 9202   20 April 1798   James Gillray
   Six brutal-looking men listen to their chairman reading of the state arrest of
   radicals. On the wall are pictures of John Horne Tooke and Thomas Paine. In
   1798 many leaders of the London Corresponding Society were arrested, a move
   clearly approved of by Gillray.

London Corresponding Society, alarm'd, Vide, Guilty Conscience

74. BMC 9214   23 May 1798   James Gillray
A serpent, with the head of Fox, tempts John Bull with the apple of reform. The trunk of the tree is 'opposition'. The tree is labelled with such fruit as 'Democracy', 'Treason', 'Plunder', 'Murder', 'Revolution', etc. The tree of justice, with very different fruit, is in the background.

The Tree of *LIBERTY*, — with, the Devil tempting John Bull.

75. BMC 9230   22 June 1798   James Gillray
Pitt and Henry Dundas whip pigs with human faces (including those of Fox, Norfolk, Bedford, Erskine, Tierney, etc.) out of an enclosure. A post bears a placard, 'London Corresponding Society – or the Cries of the Pigs in the Pound'. The leaders of the L.C.S. were arrested in 1798. Thomas Spence published a radical work entitled *Pig's Meat*, a reference to Burke's 'swinish multitude'. There are fifty lines of verse below the print.

PIGS-MEAT; or—The Swine flogg'd out of the Farm Yard.

Once a Society of Swine,
Liv'd in a Paradice of Straw,
A Herd more beautiful & fine,
I'm sure, Sir Joseph, never saw,
Of Grains, Split beans, or Pease or Swill,
Each Grunter eat & drank his fill;
You think perhaps these Pigs would bless
Their stars, for having this good Birth!
But Sages say that Happiness
Can n'er be perfect found on Earth,
And right they are, for these poor Swine,
Soon found a reason to repine;—
      A Stack Yard very tempting stood,
Near to the place, where our Pigs dwelt,
And as the Grain within seem'd good,
Each a desire to Taste it, felt;

But, ah! 'twas fenced with Paling stout,
To keep destructive Pigs without:—
      One Boar there was, with Fat opprest,
An overgrown, enormous brute,
Who long'd much more than all the rest
To ransack this forbidden Fruit,
And thus (for Pigs could then discourse)
He rav'd, until his Voice grew hoarse;
"Citizen Pigs, it grieves me much,
"To see your want of Spirit such,
"As tamely to submit to what
"The Powers above intended not,
"To be depriv'd of what we Wish,
"And not to snack the Loaves & Fish,
"Good Heav'ns! shall then the noble race
"Of Swine, endure this dire disgrace;

"Grub up for shame these Pailings vile,
"And let us every Stack despoil!—
"And this most solemnly I swear,
"Nay with the direst Oaths declare;
"If I desert the cause of Pigs,
"Or join the Wretches with two Legs
"May Nick the Dee'l, take my apostate Soul
"Down to his blackest Cinder hole!"—
      The Pigs who follow'd his advice
Grub'd up the Pales, when in a trice
Their Noses Ring'd, & Ears cut off they found,
Some, lost their Tails, & some clap'd up in Pound,
While, Timber Neckcloths clap'd on Great & Small,
Now keeps them safe, & makes them known to all,
And Johnny Bull, a gaping grins,
And cries, "poor Pigs, you suffers for your Sins
"Wounds how it makes a body Laugh,
"To see that Folks wont know; when they're well of[f]

Pub. June 22: 1798 by H. Humphrey 27 S. James Street.

76.   BMC 9286   1798?
Probably a frontispiece for an unidentified radical pamphlet. Liberty stands under a tree whose fruits are religious liberty, universal suffrage and annual parliaments. At her feet are works by Thomas Paine, William Godwin and John Thelwall. William Pitt and a Bishop are labelled with such inscriptions as taxes, slave trade, national debt, etc. They are supported by the works of Burke, etc. Below a Church and King mob duck two men in water. This is one of the rare pro-radical prints of the 1790s.

From Plague, Pestilence & Famine, from Battle & Murder & Sudden Death.

Good Lord deliver us.

HOLY BIBLE

561 FREE and unbought VOTES

Wide was the sphere of Ignorance, alas!
And faint, too faint, of Truth's young Sun the ray;
Too feeble through th' Immense of gloom to pass,
And beaming chase a world of Fog away.
P. Pindar

And they offered burnt Offerings & heave Offerings to their Gods, the Gods of Slavery, & many fell a Sacrifice. —

And the Burden was heavy on the People.

77. BMC 10372   8 March 1805   Charles Williams
Sir Francis Burdett faces Mainwaring after a very expensive election campaign
in Middlesex in 1804. Burdett castigates his opponent as a ministerial hireling,
but Mainwaring accused Burdett of bribery and corruption and was awarded
the seat in 1806. Burdett spent a huge sum contesting the Middlesex seat.

"Oh how I hate those Beams
"which bring to my remembrance from
"What State I am Fallen.

I have got a Writ of Imbarby
for Justice Juggle

Go Hireling retire to thy original
Nothingness, nor suffer Ministerial Influence
to hold theeup to ridicule again, nor dare oppose the
Legitimate Choice of the
Electors of Middlesex.

THE TRIUMPH OF INDEPENDENCE over Ministerial Influence and Corruption

Pub.d March 8.th 1806
by W.m Fores Piccadilly

Etchd by Corruptions Son
and for the Benefit
8 March 1805

78. BMC 10728   May 1807   Charles Williams
A bull is loaded down with taxes while loaves and fishes are pulled from its rump by Windham, Grenville and other Whig ministers. The ghost of Pitt claims that the ministers are pursuing the same methods as he had done. See also 36.

THE END OF PARLIAMENT

79.   BMC 10738   4 June 1807   James Gillray
The Pillar of the Constitution
Several ministerial conspirators, including Grenville, Windham, Sheridan and
Sidmouth, plot to blow up parliament. John Horne Tooke and Sir Francis
Burdett advance to take advantage of this conspiracy in order to promote the
radical cause. Gillray was favourably disposed to Canning and the Tory
opposition at this time.

80. BMC 10742   June 1807   George Woodward
A grotesque winged monster, labelled with 'Corruption', 'Sinecures', etc., attempts to corrupt John Bull who resists and tries to protect his property. In the general election both Whigs and Tories were guilty of corrupt practices. This print foreshadows the revival of reform.

THE GENIUS OF ELECTIONS or John Bulls Resolution

81. BMC 11049   1 November 1808   Samuel de Wilde
One of the earliest of many prints to attack William Cobbett. In this he is a
monstrous porcupine who fires off quills of lies and abuse. He is condemned for
changing his political views from Tory to radical. Once a supporter of the
Pittites, Cobbett has now joined his erstwhile opponents Burdett and Horne
Tooke, who are also depicted as monsters.

The PORCUPINE'S Den.

Published for the Satirist Nov.r 1 1808 by S.r W. Fores 37 Leadenhall Street

82. BMC 11211   1 January 1809   Samuel de Wilde
Robin Hood Debating Societies had existed in many towns since the mid-eighteenth century. They usually favoured a greater measure of political liberty. In this satire on their activities ruffianly fellows gather around a table. Pockets are being picked and the spoils handed to a man on a rostrum. Among the members of the Society is John Gale Jones, a prominent radical, who was imprisoned for his activities. The debating society in this print is in fact more likely to be the British Forum, rather than a Robin Hood Society.

The ROBBING Hood Debating Society.

Published for the Satirist Jan'ry 1809. by S. Tipper 37 Leadenhall Street

1 Jan. 1809.

83. BMC 11328   1 May 1809   Samuel de Wilde
Several radicals, including Burdett, Horne Tooke, Folkestone and Whitbread, attack Britannia. Cobbett approaches as a porcupine. Above Britannia an eagle with the crowned head of Napoleon hovers menacingly. This was published in the *Satirist*. The radicals had moved for a committee to enquire into corrupt practices on 17 April 1709.

A SECOND SIGHT View of the BLESSINGS of RADICAL REFORM. see page 118
Published for the National Mag.t 1809 by S.T. Tipper 37 Leadenhall street

84. BMC 11332   28 May 1809   Thomas Rowlandson
A monster of corruption addresses John Bull. The monster opposes reform, but John Bull shows some support for the idea of reform. This print indicates the revival of reform at this time.

IOHN BULL AND THE GENIUS OF CORRUPTION.

Pod.^d May 28.th 1809 by Th.^s Tegg N.¹¹¹ Cheapside

85. BMC 11338   14 June 1809   James Gillray
    Sir Francis Burdett, aided by several radicals including Horne Tooke,
    Whitbread and Cobbett, incites a mob to destroy parliament and to overthrow
    the constitution. Two corrupt opposition Whigs, Grenville and Buckingham,
    hurry off. Parliament is attacked in the background.

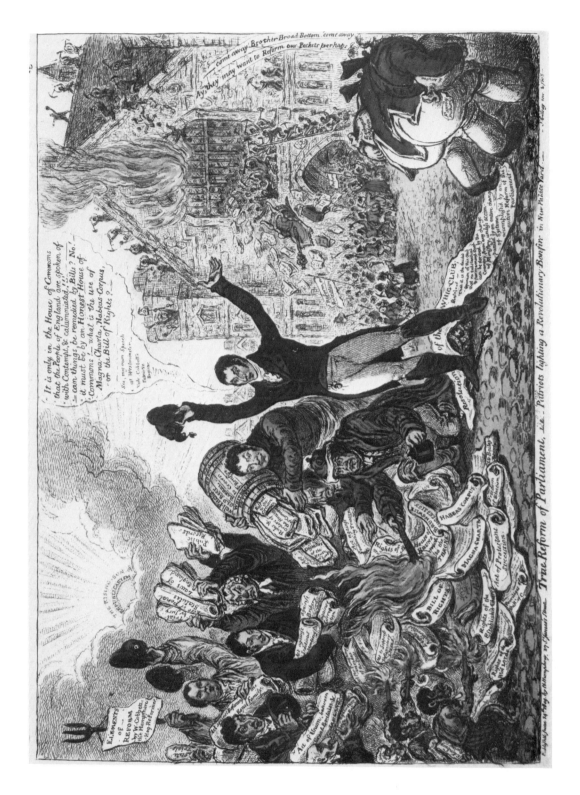

True Reform of Parliament, i.e. — Patriots lighting a Revolutionary Bonfire in New Palace Yard. —

86.   BMC 11531   February 1810   Isaac Cruikshank
      This is one of the rare prints which is favourable towards Sheridan. He is praised
      on this occasion for defending the liberty of the press in a speech on 6 February
      1810. The caricaturists were usually strong defenders of a free press. In this print
      Sheridan defends the press from a monstrous spirit of corruption which hurls
      darts at him. His shield is inscribed 'Liberty of the Press'.

THE CHAMPION of LIBERTY.

87. BMC 11537   1 April 1810   William Heath

John Bull is knocked down by a large red book entitled 'a list of pensions and sinecures for the year 1810'. The book is attacked by three reformers: Whitbread, Burdett, and Calcraft (a barrister). Horne Tooke is encouraging them. This print illustrates the continued interest of radicals in parliamentary reform.

AN ATTACK on le LIVRE·ROUGE; or Champions of Liberty ridiculing an overgrown Red Book

88.   BMC 11538   6 April 1810   William Heath
Sir Francis Burdett, in armour, attacks a seven-headed monster which guards
the Treasury. The monster's heads represent ministers including Perceval,
Lethbridge, Croker and Windham. Burdett had opposed the decision of the
House of Commons to arrest John Gale Jones. He was himself ordered to be
committed to the Tower on 6 April.

Modern St George Attacking the Monster of Despotism

89. BMC 11560   May 1810   Charles Williams

Sir Francis Burdett pushes over two pillars of parliament labelled 'Corrupt Representation' and 'Unlawful Privilege'. The ministers above, including Perceval, Lethbridge and Yorke are fearful. Burdett is aided by Lord Cochrane, his fellow radical M.P. for Westminster, and Gwllym Lloyd Wardle, who had started the campaign against the sale of army commissions by the mistress of the Duke of York. Burdett was imprisoned in the Tower in 1810 for challenging the right of the House of Commons to gaol John Gale Jones for criticising their decision to exclude strangers from the chamber. Burdett was immensely popular in 1810 – on the scale of John Wilkes forty years before.

THE POLITICAL SAMPSON or Philistines in Danger

90. BMC 11707   January 1811   George Cruikshank
Ministers, including Eldon, Perceval and Lethbridge, are shown in the elaborate interior of the Treasury where they are scooping up gold and coins. Castlereagh and Canning are quarrelling. This is a satire on ministerial corruption.

STATE MINERS.

91. BMC 11923   1812?   William Elmes

Two grotesquely ugly parliamentary candidates seek the vote of a sturdy, ragged ratcatcher, who refuses to vote for the candidates because the candidates will not offer him a large enough bribe and have previously jailed him for poaching. This is a satire on the political morality of both candidates and electors.

CANDIDATES "Canvasing" for Seats in Parliament.

92. BMC 12037   19 April 1813   George Cruikshank
A sturdy John Bull, ragged and shackled, faces tax collectors who are demanding yet more taxes.

A FREE BORN ENGLISHMAN!—
THE PRIDE OF THE WORLD!
AND THE ENVY OF SURROUNDING NATIONS!!!.

93. BMC 12503   3 March 1815   George Cruikshank
This satire attacks the recently passed Corn Laws which prevented the import of cheap foreign corn in order to protect the landed interest. In this print four landlords on shore turn back a French boat loaded with cheap corn. They are ready to see the poor starve rather than reduce the price of corn. The Corn Laws reached their second reading on 3 March.

The Blessings of Peace or the Curse of the Corn Bill.

94. BMC 12786   c. June 1816   Charles Williams
    John Bull, in patched and ragged clothes, bends under the weight of the military
    establishment, including forts, soldiers and cannons. There was much
    discontent at the size of the military establishment even after the end of the long
    and expensive war with France.

THE BRITISH ATLAS, or John Bull supporting the Peace Establishment.

95. BMC 12819   4 December 1816   Robert? Cruikshank
Henry Hunt, the leading radical orator of the age, holds the Petition of Right
and urges the use of moral pressure rather than physical force. This refers to
part of Hunt's speech at Spa Fields, London, on 15 November 1816. It is one of
the very few prints which is not sharply hostile to Hunt.

THE SPA FIELDS HUNT-ER
OR
A PATRIOT MOUNTED.

96. BMC 12863   January 1817   Charles Williams
British households, represented as beehives, are attacked by swarms of tax-collectors. John Bull defies them with a pitchfork inscribed 'Prop of Reform'. He is aided by his wife who wields a poker. This is a satire on the heavy taxation and widespread distress of 1816–17.

Quarter Day

N.º 1. BLESSINGS of BRITAIN— or — Swarm of Tax-Gatherers. "All quite united force comayne to Draw."
The lazy Drones from the laborer's Hive." Virgil

97. BMC 12864   8 February 1817   George Cruikshank
John Bull, as a bull, is pursued by a radical mob (led by Cobbett, Lord
Cochrane, Henry Hunt and Major John Cartwright) and by ministerial
butchers (including the Prince Regent, Vansittart, Eldon, Liverpool and
Castlereagh). Ellenborough stands in a sentry box with the word 'Law' on his
bayonet. This satire is a version of 'a plague on both your houses'.

HUNT=ing the BULL!?!

London Pub.d Feb.y 8.th 1817
by J. Sidebotham, 1. St. James's.

98.   BMC 12867   26 February 1817   George Cruikshank
Henry Brougham, a Whig supporter of moderate reform, uses a fire extinguisher against the radical Lord Cochrane, who stands on a gas container which also has Cobbett, Hunt and (perhaps) Thomas Evans, and serpents on it. Demons stoke up the furnace with radical works. The quotations are from Brougham's speech against universal suffrage on 14 February 1817. This was one of the most damaging of the anti-radical prints.

A PATRIOT LUMINARY EXTINGUISHING NOXIOUS GAS !!! ———

99. BMC 12869   1 March 1817   George Cruikshank
Henry Hunt is shown as a demagogue addressing a crowd from the window of a
public house. There are placards in favour of reform and also of anarchy. The
crowd are ragged and ruffianly. Hunt addressed a meeting on 10 February 1817.
Below the design there are several verses.

The Stu: fields Orator HUNT-ing for Popularity to DO=GOOD!! —

"The State is out of tune, distracting fears
And jealous Envoils jar on our, public Counsels
A midst the wealthy City, murmurs rise
Loud railings & reproach on those that rule,
With open storm of Government, menace crude

Cruel, hard to trust 'twixt man & man are broke,
The golden streams of commerce are with-held
Which feed the wants of needy hands & Artizans
Who therefore Curse the great word Threat Rebellion"

BLITHE HARRY HUNT was an Orator bold!
Talk'd away bravely and blunt;
And Rome in her glory and Athens of old,
With all their loud talkers of whom we are told,
Could n't match Orator HUNT!

Blythe HARRY HUNT was a slighty man,
Something 'twixt giant and runt;
His paunch was a large one, his visage was wan,
And to hear his long speeches vast multitudes ran.
O rare Orator HUNT!

He hated a pension, he hated a place;
Gave them a groan and a grunt;
Call'd Ministers *Villains,* and Crowns *a Disgrace;*
And wish'd to cut short the monarchical race.
O rare Orator HUNT!

Orator HUNT he could both read and write,
Meagre his mind tho' and stunt;
His knowledge of grammar indeed was so slight,
That a sentence of English he couldn't indite.
O rare Orator HUNT!

How Orator HUNT's many speeches will close,
Tedious, bombastic, and blunt,
In a halter or diadem, God only knows;
The sequel might well an arch-conjuror pose
O rare Orator HUNT!

100. BMC 12871   1817   George Cruikshank
Castlereagh, Eldon and Ellenborough, the most conservative of the Tory ministers, are shown astride a dismantled printing press. They show sinecurists and pensioners the hanging body of Liberty which is clutching Magna Carta, the Bill of Rights and Habeas Corpus, and which is gagged with the recently passed 'Gagging Bill'. John Bull weeps on a hill where he stands with leading radicals, including Cochrane, Cobbett, Hunt and Burdett. George Cruikshank was not always pro-radical, but he always favoured freedom of expression.

LIBERTY SUSPENDED! with the Bulwark of the Constitution?

101. BMC 12891   October 1817   George Cruikshank
This print originated in an idea from an amateur. On 21 August 1817 Robert
Owen, at a meeting in London, put forward his 'Plan of Amelioration and
Reformation without Revolution', which proposed the setting up of villages of
unity and co-operation. Various radicals, including Robert Waithman,
William Hone, Thomas Wooler and John Cartwright, reply by insisting that
the widespread distress can only be cured by political reform.

A Peep into the City of LONDON TAVERN, by an Irish Amateur on the 21st of August 1817.

Or, A Sample of the Co-operation to be expected in one of Mr OWEN's Projected Paradises.

102. BMC 13001   3 July 1818   Robert Cruikshank
Henry Hunt is shown presiding at a meeting of revolutionary conspirators. He wears tricolour favours and drinks blood. A guillotine is behind him. The ruffianly group include John Gale Jones, Thomas Wooler, and the Spencean revolutionaries Arthur Thistlewood, Thomas Preston and James Watson. The latter group supported Hunt for the Westminster constituency in June 1818.

Modern Reformers in Council.—or—Patriots Regaling

103. BMC 13002   7 July 1818   Robert Cruikshank
Sir Francis Burdett defends the people of the land of misery and oppression
against a swarm of monsters. He is dressed in liberty and carries a sword of
flame inscribed with the names of Thomas Wooler, John Cartwright, William
Hone, Robert Waithman, etc. Burdett defends Hunt, Maxwell, Ellenborough,
Sir William Curtis, etc. He is therefore in favour of moderate reform but
hostile to the radical extremists and the Tories, especially in the election for
Westminster.

The CHAMPION of Westminster: defending the People from Ministerial Imps. & Reptiles.

104. BMC 13248   17 July 1819   George Cruikshank
A many-headed monster, the symbol of revolution, stands on a pile of
emblems, including the crown, coronets, a mitre, the scales of justice, Magna
Carta, etc.

Universal Suffrage. or. the Scum Uppermost ___ !!!!

An Allegory, to demonstrate the fatal consequences of "Radical Reform"
in plain English REVOLUTION _____

105. BMC 13252   July 1819   Charles Williams
Henry Hunt addresses a meeting of reformers at Smithfield on 21 July 1819.
His head is that of an ass, while his audience are cattle, sheep, horses and pigs,
all of them on their hind legs. See also BMC 13253.

THE SMITHFIELD PARLIAMENT. i.e Universal Suffrage.— the New Speaker addressing the Members.

106. BMC 13257   1819   George Cruikshank
This satire on female radicals was produced for the conservative George Humphrey. It was based on a report of female radicals attending a meeting at Blackburn on 5 July which was printed in Thomas Wooler's *Black Dwarf* on 14 July. Cruikshank turns the political threat into a sexual joke. All the radicals shown are from the lower orders. A file of female radicals present a cap of liberty to the chairman of a reform meeting.

The Belle-alliance, or the Female Reformers of Blackburn !!!

107. BMC 13258   16 August 1819   Robert or George Cruikshank
An attack on the violent disruption of the radical meeting at St. Peter's Field, Manchester, that became known as 'Peterloo'. Fat yeomanry are shown savagely riding over men, women and children. Peterloo helped turn public opinion against the Tory government and make it more sympathetic to reform. The print was produced on the very day of the incident in Manchester.

Massacre at St Peters or "BRITONS STRIKE HOME"!!!

108. BMC 13271   17 September 1819   George Cruikshank
The heads of the political nation (the Prince Regent, Liverpool, Castlereagh and Eldon), dropping bags of money, flee from a grotesque monster whose body is a guillotine and which holds daggers and sends flames after the fugitives. Tiny guillotine reformers join the chase.

A Radical Reformer,—(ie) a Neck-or-nothing man! Dedicated to the Heads of the Nation.

109. BMC 13279 1 December 1819 George Cruikshank
Death, wearing the mask of liberty, tries to ravish Britannia, who is braced against the rock of religion and brandishes the sword of the laws. Death's cloak is inscribed 'radical reform' and Death is aided by imps and demons with such labels as 'Murder', 'Starvation', 'Robbery', 'Blasphemy', etc. The British lion approaches to defend Britannia.

THE LAWS

RELIGION

RADICAL REFORM

'DEATH or LIBERTY'. or Britannia & the Virtues of the Constitution in danger of Violation, from the gr.^t Political Libertine, Radical Reform.'

110. BMC 13283   December 1819   Robert Cruikshank
William Cobbett, astride a diabolical monster and followed by demons,
returns to England where he is welcomed by a mob. Cobbett had fled to the
United States in 1817 because he had feared arrest for his political writings.
He returned in 1819, bringing with him the bones of Thomas Paine who had
been buried in New York State. He arrived at Liverpool on 21 November.
This print indicates that the Americans were pleased to see the back of him.

The Political CHAMPION turned Resurrection Man!

W. COBBETT

111. BMC 13288   15 December 1819   George Cruikshank
A bull, muzzled with the gagging bill, collapses under a massive burden of
bishops, ministers, officers, tax collectors, etc. Wellington is the bull's
executioner. Cruikshank was often opposed to radical political reform, but
usually favoured economical reform. A similar print appeared in 1826 (BMC
15363). The satire was aimed at taxation, corruption and militarism.

Poor BULL & his Burden — or the Political MURRAION !!!
"And the land stank — so num'rous was the fry."
— What will become of these Vermin, if the Bull should Rise — ? !!!!!!!!!!!

Pub.d Dec.r 8 1819 by J.Fogg 11 Cheapside London.

G Cruick.k fec.t

15 Dec 1819

112. BMC 13504   15 January 1820   George Cruikshank
This is the frontispiece to a verse satire on the repressive nature of the recently-passed Six Acts. John Bull is shackled, padlocked, gagged, etc. Magna Carta and the Bill of Rights are pierced by a bloody dagger. Bulky papers, inscribed 'six new acts', are on John Bull's head. On top of the papers sits Castlereagh like a bird of prey. Cruikshank regularly defended the civil liberties of the subject without necessarily supporting radical reform.

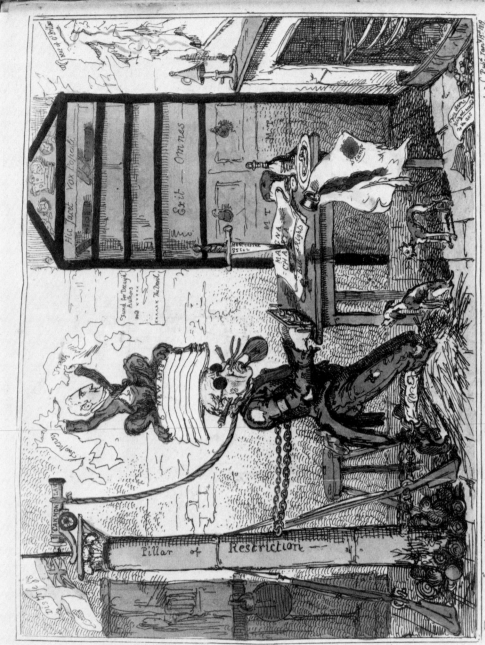

Poor John Bull - The Free Born Englishman - Deprived of his Seven Senses. By the Six New Acts?

113. BMC 13508   January 1820   George Cruikshank
The Prince Regent, on the moon, tries to obscure the sun with a blanket on his sword. A comet rushes towards him. Its head is a cap of liberty, its tail 'reform'. This burlesque on the Regent's opposition to reform illustrated a verse satire by the radical publisher William Hone. It reached its 51st edition by 1821 and was followed by a whole series of small woodcuts exemplifying it.

THE
MAN IN THE MOON
&c. &c. &c.

" If Cæsar can hide the Sun with a blanket, or put the Moon in his pocket,
we will pay him tribute for light."—*Cymbeline.*

WITH FIFTEEN CUTS.

LONDON:
PRINTED BY AND FOR WILLIAM HONE,
45, LUDGATE HILL.

1820.

ONE SHILLING.

114. BMC 13556   1820
     The temple of the constitution has three columns of King, Lords and
     Commons. On the dome Britannia replaces Liberty. Within the temple the
     King is enthroned between Justice and a parson. A short verse praises the
     constitution and plenty. The next print (BMC 13557), on the benefits of
     radical reform, has the palace shattered, corn on fire, a ship sinking, while
     Britannia has disappeared.

THE PALACE OF JOHN BULL.

See the **KINGS** solid pillar the centre unites,
And the **LORDS** and the **COMMONS** uphold British rights.
Round the Palace fields wave with abundance of corn,
And the reapers sing joyful o'er plenty's full horn.
While **SHIPS** heavy laden with India's treasures;
Enter port to regale us & heighten our pleasures.

115. BMC 13707 9 March 1820 George Cruikshank
This is the famous print showing the Bow Street officers arresting the Spencean conspirators in their stable loft at Cato Street on 23 February 1820. The conspirators had planned to assassinate the Cabinet at dinner. The leading conspirator, Arthur Thistlewood, actually escaped but was captured next day. He and four others were later executed and another five were transported for life.

The **CATO STREET CONSPIRATORS**, on the Memorable Night of the 23rd of Feby 1820. at the moment when Smithers the Police officer was stabbed; N.B The Scene faithfully represented, from the Description of Mr Ruthven, the View of the Interior correctly Sketched, on the Spot ——

116.   BMC 13710   23 April 1820   George Cruikshank
This print, 'showing the necessity of reform in the close boroughs', reveals inhabitants being evicted from a small borough for not voting as ordered by the patron of the borough. The borough Cruikshank had in mind is that of Tregony, which had recently been bought by Lord Darlington. It is one of the rare prints actually exploring the defects of the electoral system.

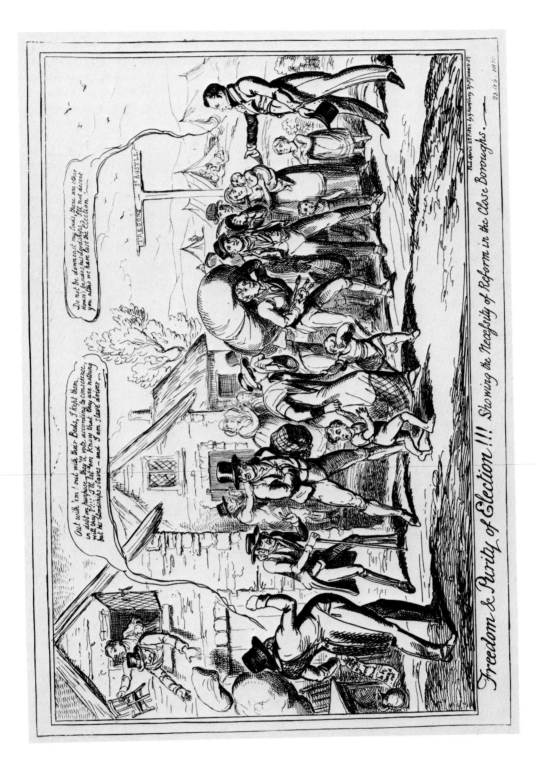

Freedom & Purity of Election !!! Showing the Necessity of Reform in the Close Boroughs.

117. BMC 13713   May 1820
A gang of Tory ministers (Sidmouth, Castlereagh, Gifford, Canning, Vansittart and Abbott) dance around a pole on which are the heads of the Cato Street conspirators. George Edwards, the government agent provocateur who had betrayed the conspiracy, plays a fiddle and claims, 'Dance away my Friends, I have been the cause of all this fun by your help and money'. This print shows that there was some sympathy for the fate of the conspirators and some hostility for the tactics of the ministry.

"Dance away my Friends, I have been the cause of all this fun by your Help and Money. "Edwards the Instigator""!!!

A MAY DAY GARLAND for 1820.

Pub. May 1820 by J.W. Fores 41 Piccadilly Corner.

118. BMC 13714   25 May 1820   George Cruikshank

John Bull, with both legs amputated (one peg leg is inscribed 'Universal Suffrage', the other 'Religious Freedom'), is being bled by Sir Francis Burdett, while John Cam Hobhouse, another radical M.P., offers him a drink. John Bull's pillow is labelled 'False Promises' and 'Reformers Opinions'; his armchair is labelled 'Mistaken Security' and 'Mistaken Confidence'. Various medicines are labelled with the names of radicals.

RADICAL QUACKS giving a New Constitution to John Bull.!

119. BMC 13895   October 1820   George Cruikshank

Queen Caroline leads the radicals up a ladder to attack the crown and constitution. The pillar is labelled King, Lords and Commons. The rungs of the ladder are labelled with the names of various radical disturbances (such as the Spa Fields Riot, Peterloo, and the Cato Street Conspiracy). The back of the ladder reads Revolution, Anarchy and Ruin. Queen Caroline had been immensely popular during her trial, but this print marks the beginning of the reaction against her and her radical supporters. This print appeared in *The Loyalists' Magazine*.

The RADICAL LADDER.

London Pub.d by G Humphrey 27 St James's St April 15 1821

120. BMC 14194   June or July 1821   Robert Cruikshank
The Revolutionary Association
The radical leaders are flanked by revolutionary mobs. Waithman and Wood, both with ass's ears, are on a platform. Behind them William Hone declares 'No King, no Church, no order on the face of the earth'. An ostrich, with the head of Sir Francis Burdett, addresses the crowd. Arthur Thistlewood and Richard Watson plan to burn London. Richard Carlile, Henry Hunt and Thomas Wooler are also present. Robert Cruickshank and his brother George are both included in the print in which they pore over drawings.

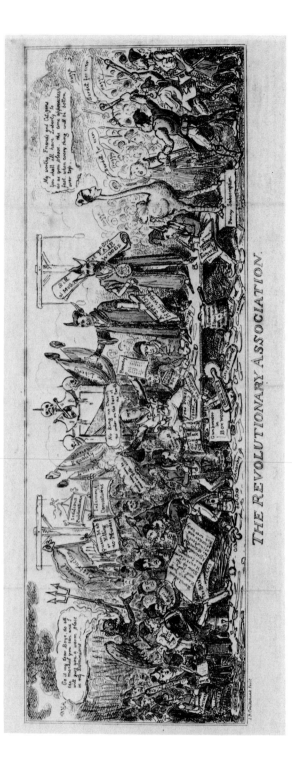

THE REVOLUTIONARY ASSOCIATION.

121.	BMC 15497	c. January 1828	Robert Seymour
John Bull, while very ill in bed, is beset by phantoms. A demon, labelled 'National Debt', sits on his chest. At the foot of his bed Eldon and Wellington oppose changes to the Corn Laws. Henry Hunt is a top hat inscribed 'radical reform' and a monstrous head is labelled 'Popery'. A black skeleton leans over the bed, supported on the works of Thomas Paine. Two arms labelled 'bankruptcy hammer' threaten to strike John Bull's head with a hammer. This print reveals all the perils facing the ordinary subject – an oppressive ministry, dangerous radicals, Catholic demands and an economic depression.

BANKRUPTCY HAMMER

WIGG BALSAM

J. BULL

COMMERCIAL LEDGERS

800000000

NATIONAL DEBT.

POPERY

RADICAL REFORM

FOREIGN CORN.

JOHN BULL'S NIGHT MARE.

to keep he always dreams of one or more
When this unfortunate feel, (having nothing   of these length Spectres sometimes of all her ties
to keep him awake) retires after a hearty meal

122.   BMC 15530   c. April 1828   William Heath

This is the only print about the repeal of the Test and Corporation Acts. Peers and bishops battle on horseback with bladders on poles. Wellington, aided by Holland and Grey who fight under the banner of 'civil and religious liberty', defeats the reactionary forces (led by Lord Eldon) which support 'Bigotry', 'Protestant Ascendancy' and 'Church in Danger'.

The GRAND BATTLE of LORDS SPIRITUAL and TEMPORAL or Political courage brought to the TEST.

Debate on repeal of Test Act.

April 17. 1828.

123. BMC 15682   March 1829

A large pair of scales are labelled 'Public Opinion'. On one side is 'Liberality' and 'March of Intellect'. Daniel O'Connell, newspapers (especially *The Times*), and the devil pull it down to the pit of hell. Two rats, one of whom is Robert Peel, climb up the rope to this scale. In the second scale there is Eldon, Britannia's shield, '1688', the constitution, other newspapers and clergy helping. Below William Cobbett stands on a bridge asking which way he should turn. Catholic Emancipation was secured in 1829, aided by the desertion of Peel and Wellington. Cobbett had recently quarrelled with O'Connell and he disliked this particular bill, while sympathising with the Catholics.

MARCH 1820

124. BMC 15687   c. March 1829
Eldon defends the constitution, behind a barricade of petitions, against the combined forces of the Tories Wellington and Peel, the radical Burdett, the Whig Henry Brougham, the Irish champion Daniel O'Connell, etc., who ride over Magna Carta, the Protestant succession, etc. The pillars of the constitution are inscribed 'King', 'Lords' and 'Commons'.

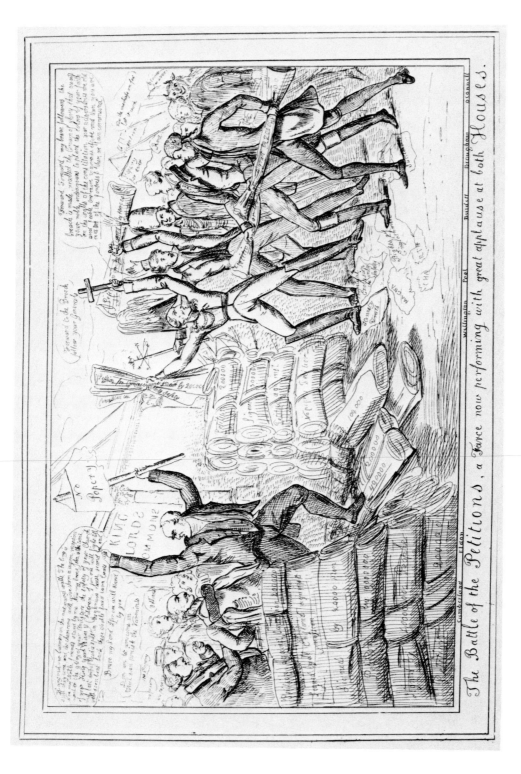

The Battle of the Petitions, a Farce now performing with great applause at both Houses.

125. BMC 15799   10 June 1829   Robert Seymour?
Clinging to a broken shaft labelled 'Manufactures & Commerce' are four
ragged and desperate artisans. Two larger employers cling to the artisans and
clinging to the employers is a very large figure – half king, half bishop –
labelled 'Church and State'. Manufacture and commerce, both in a depressed
state in 1829, are seen as the supporters of the whole nation but are threatened
by the heavy financial burden imposed by Church and State.

Manufactures & Commerce support the Workmen
they the Merchants & Masters who are the
chief tax payers & thereby support
The great tax eater Church-and-State.

MANUFACTURES & COMMERCE

STATE OF THE NATION. *"An over true Tale"*

126. BMC 15884   13 October 1829   HB = John Doyle
The Duke of Newcastle and Michael Sadler, the Duke's nominee for his borough of Newark, evict a tenant who has dared to vote against Sadler and for his opponent, Wilde. Newcastle later defended his action in the House of Lords in December 1830. During the riots of 1831 a mob took revenge on Newcastle and burned down his castle at Nottingham.

XXVIII.

NEWCASTLE versus NEWARK.

Published by T. McLean, 26 Haymarket, Oct 13. 1829.

127. BMC 16073   20 March 1830   William Heath
John Bull is rained upon by cats, dogs and pitchforks inscribed with the names of various taxes. They stick into him, his dog and his umbrella which is labelled 'trade'.

POOR Mr BULL IN A PRETTY SITUATION — *For the Rain it Raineth every day*

RAINING-CATS-DOGS-&-PITCHFORKS with the PRONGS DOWNWARD
It must be the fault of the Weather—for when it rains—it rains Taxes—& when it shines—it shines Taxes—
Pub March 20 1830 by T. McLean 26 Haymarket London

128. BMC 16166   14 July 1830   Robert Seymour
Some borough constituencies had a wide franchise in which the right to vote
was possessed by every male inhabitant who could boil his own pot. These
potwallopers were urged by the reformers to exercise their vote in order to
strengthen the independent element in the House of Commons. In this satire a
ragged, disreputable potwalloper is asked to vote for an independent
candidate, but the tramp takes more notice of a man who offers him a bribe
for his vote.

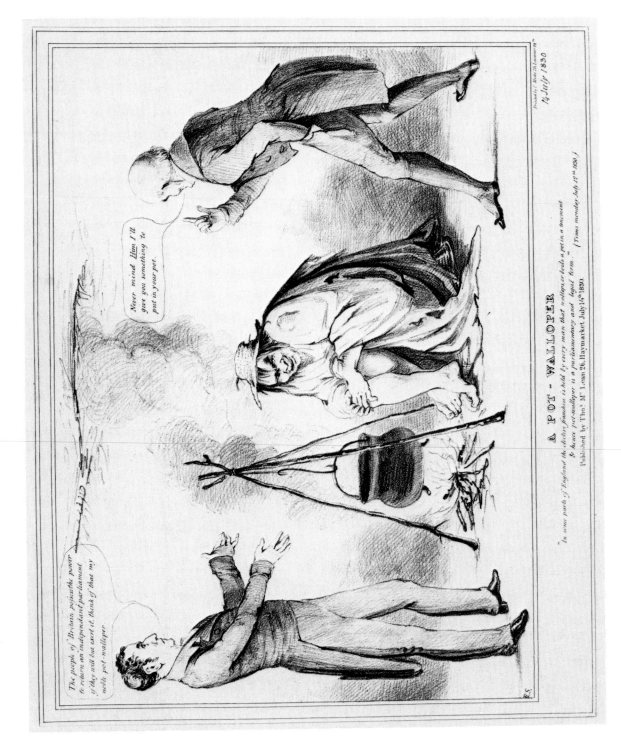

A POT - WALLOPER

"In some parts of England the electors franchise is held by every man that wollops or boils a pot in a tenement & hence pot-walloper is a parliamentary and legal term." (Times tuesday July 12th 1830)

Published by Thos. McLean 26. Haymarket July 14th 1830.

129.   BMC 16170   19 July 1830   William Heath

A borough patron, with a rope around the necks of the electors, offers to sell them to a candidate.

Election Squibs & Crackers – N.º 2

Here they are all good votes – ready to vote for my coach horse, if I order them – give me the money & I'll secure you the seat

Well, here's the Cash, as for the votes I'll leave them to you

HOW TO GET MADE AN M P !!!

130. BMC 16286   October 1830?

This lithograph shows a goose hatching the eggs of Reform, Common Rights and Small Farms and expressing delight that William IV favours reform. The bust portraits of Peel and Wellington show contempt for reform and for the widespread distress of the people. The King shows that he is disposed to oppose Peel and Wellington and ready to listen to the appeals of his distressed people. This is one of the very few prints associating the distress caused by the enclosure of commons and the amalgamation of farms with the demand for parliamentary reform.

REFORM and COMMON RIGHTS. Just Hatched.

Pub.d by M.Phillips; 12, Water St. Blackfriars.

1832.

131. BMC 16289 1 November 1830 Robert Seymour
This print appeared in *The Looking Glass*. A large elector, liberated by being able to vote in secret, kicks a peer, who staggers back snorting 'Boroughs to Sell' and 'Impotent Rage'. This is a rare print in favour of the secret ballot, a reform not passed in fact until 1872.

THE SPIRIT OF ARISTOCRACY
RECEVING A
VOTE BY BALLOT !!!

132. BMC 16404   c. December 1830   George Cruikshank
Swing
In 1830 there were widespread riots, known as the Swing riots, by agricultural labourers. Cruikshank compares the political radicals with these rioters. William Cobbett and Henry Hunt lead the rioters, who use radical works as torches, in burning a crowned haystack inscribed with 'religion' and 'the constitution'.

133. BMC 16573   1 February 1831   Robert Seymour
This appeared in McLean's *Monthly Sheet of Caricatures*. A judge sentences two peers, the Marquis of Exeter and the Duke of Newcastle, who have been convicted as boroughmongers. He ridicules their demand for compensation for the loss of the right of representation by the small boroughs which they controlled. Compensation was not given in the 1832 Bill, although it had been part of Pitt's Bill of 1785 and the Irish borough patrons had been compensated after the Act of Union in 1800.

AGITATORS AGITATED!!! ON THEIR TRIP'S TO LIVERPOOL.

Recommended to the Great OC— & the rest of them as the best way of disposing of themselves for the good of their Country. (Steam boiler's have burst & may again)

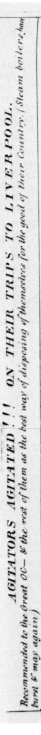

Talk of wanting compensation because you are deprived of your plunder,
why you are the most impudent thieves that ever come before me, But as the
prosecutor John Bull was much to blame for suffering himself to be so pillaged
I shall pass but a light sentence — I therefore ordain that you each be
branded on the forehead with the letter C.B. signifying Convicted Bo-rou-mon-g-s

BOROUGHMONGERS BROUGHT TO THE BAR!!
or the question of compensation.

Printed by C. Motte 23. Leicester

134. BMC 16584   26 February 1831   Robert Seymour
Earl Grey and Lord Althorp, as magicians, raise a devil which they cannot lay
again. Grey stands aghast at a demon wearing a Jacobin cap of liberty, with
'Reform' on its horns and 'Revolution' on its forehead. The demon breathes fire
and smoke and the words 'Vote by Ballot, Universal Suffrage, No Tythes, No
Lords, No —'. The implication of the satire is that the moderate measure
proposed by the Whigs will inevitably lead to much more radical reforms.

THE CUNNING MEN.

They have raised a Devil they cannot lay again.

Published by Thos M:Lean 26, Haymarket, February 26th 1851.

135. BMC 16606　12 March 1831　Sharpshooter?
Earl Grey and Henry Brougham, with the weapons of 'Reform', attack a hydra of corruption which has seven Tory heads (Peel, Wellington, Eldon, Cumberland, Aberdeen, Wetherell and Bathurst). William IV stands behind Grey and Brougham.

Pub.d by G.Humphrey 24 S.t James's Street. March 12. 1821.

The Champions of Reform destroying the Monster of Corruption

136.   BMC 16610   21 March 1831   George Cruikshank
One of the most famous and effective prints. The House of Commons is
depicted as a decayed mill. A large spout from one end delivers gold to tax
eaters. The flow is labelled 'pensions', 'places', 'preferments', 'contracts', etc.
The mill wheel is inscribed with the names of rotten boroughs. Dying bodies
lie under the 'system'. The print is a comprehensive indictment of ministerial
corruption and the defects of the electoral system.

"The System that Works so Well!" — or The Boroughmongers GRINDING Machine —

137.   BMC 16618   31 March 1831   Charles Grant
Four orators give their views on the advisability of reform. Grey presents the
Whig view, Wellington the Tory view, John Lee the 'liberal' view, and Cobbett
the radical view. It is an interesting assessment of the conflicting opinions on
the Reform Bill. See also (*141*).

FOUR WEIGHTY AUTHORITIES ON REFORM.

138.   BMC 16634   13 April 1831   HB = John Doyle
Grey and Brougham leapfrog over the King, who is losing his crown, and
Wellington. Other Whigs also make a mess of leapfrogging over judges and
bishops. Lord Lansdowne sprawls over Eldon. Radicals at the top of the hill
(including Burdett, Hunt and O'Connell) cheer. This satire on the effects of
reform on the crown and other institutions implies that William IV was not
favourably disposed towards the Reform Bill.

LEAP FROG.
Down Constitution Hill.

London: Published by Thos. McLean, 26, Haymarket, April 5th 1831.

139. BMC 16643   28 April 1831

In the House of Commons Lord Durham urges on Lord John Russell (the promoter of the Reform Bill), who is feeding such documents as Magna Carta and the Bill of Rights into the head of a monster. From this head project numerous past and present radicals including Wilkes, Junius, Hunt, Cobbett, Brougham and Paine. The Reform Bill is clearly seen as a sop to the radicals whose appetite will not be satisfied with such a measure.

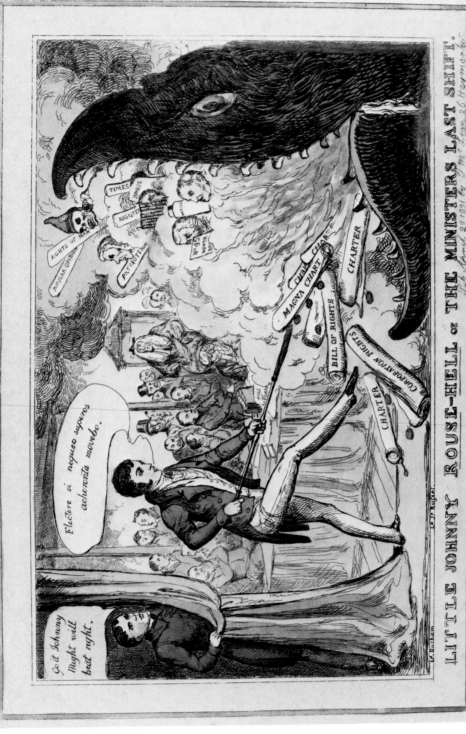

LITTLE JOHNNY ROUSE-HELL or THE MINISTERS LAST SHIFT.

140. BMC 16650   April 1831?   Sharpshooter?
A group of reformers, including Brougham, Grey, Lansdowne, Althorp, Burdett and Thomas Attwood, chop down a decayed tree which bears the names of rotten boroughs. A number of leading anti-reformers, including Peel, Wellington, Scarlett, Ellenborough, Newcastle and Chandos, attempt to prop up the tree. On a distant 'Constitution' hill stand the King, the Queen, John Bull, Pat (a symbol for the Irish) and Sandy (a symbol for the Scots).

The Reformers' Attack on the Old Rotten Trees; or, the Foul Nests of the Cormorants in Danger.

141. BMC 16756 1 August 1831 Robert Seymour

This print appeared in McLean's *Monthly Sheet of Caricatures*. It is similar to (*137*). Interesting comments on the Reform Bill are being made by a radical reformer, a supporter of the Bill, a bit-by-bit reformer, and an anti-reformer. The second speaker appears to be the most sensible and respectable of the four.

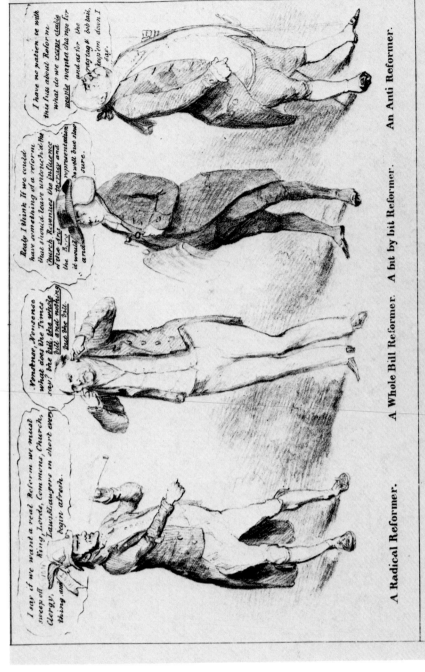

A Radical Reformer.   A Whole Bill Reformer.   A bit by bit Reformer.   An Anti Reformer.

FOUR SPECIMENS OF THE POLITICAL PUBLICK.

Printed by C. Hunt 79 S Marian Lane.

142. BMC 16781 1 October 1831 Robert Seymour
This print is from McLean's *Monthly Sheet of Caricatures*. Inside a lock Tory peers are attempting to stop a flood of water which is inscribed with the word 'Reform'. They use buckets with such inappropriate labels as 'piety', 'humility', 'eloquence' and 'liberality'. The peers are Londonderry, Eldon, Cumberland, Wellington, Ellenborough and perhaps Northumberland. Watching from the bank are Brougham, Grey and William IV.

Vol. 2

Oct.r 1.st
1831.

Mr. LEAN'S MONTHLY SHEET OF CARICATURES N.o 22

Prize 3.s Plain.
6. Col.d

DR. THE COMING GRASS.

PUBLISHED ON THE FIRST OF EVERY MONTH.

I've set open the Flood Gates and if
they are simple enough to place themselves
in its way, they do it, at their own peril.

NOBLE LORDS OPPOSING THE TORRENT OF REFORM.

"Let your means be adequate to the end proposed."

143. BMC 16821   c. November 1831   I. Brooks?
This print shows three entrances to the House of Commons. The archway on the left is a narrow tunnel labelled 'Corporation Entrance' and Robert Peel is paying to enter. The centre archway, placarded with the words 'Independent Entrance', has Sir Francis Burdett entering. The archway on the right is the 'Common Sewer Entrance' which has the head of the Duke of Newcastle above it. Sir Charles Wetherell is entering through this archway. Peel and Wetherell were arch-defenders of the small boroughs in the debates on the Reform Bill. Burdett was the member for Westminster, Peel for Westbury and Wetherell for Boroughbridge.

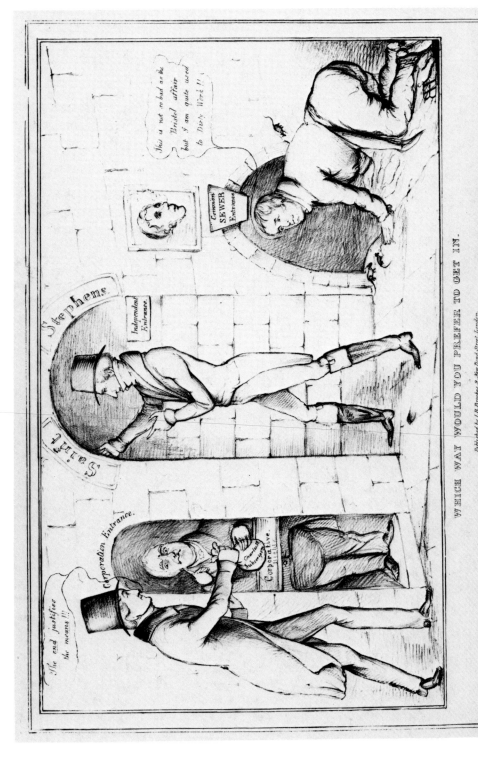

144. BMC 16991   12 April 1832   HB = John Doyle
Lord Grey is shown about to step off a cliff into a rocky abyss inscribed 'Reform'. He is being pushed by Lord Durham, who is arm-in-arm with Brougham. Other cabinet ministers are behind them. Demons and demagogues beckon them on. Over their heads are extended many newspapers with thin threads leading from them to the shoulders of the ministers. Doyle is attacking the excessive influence of the press and public opinion on the Whigs that is leading the ministers into dangerous extremism.

THE UNITED CABINET.
OR
THE BLIND LEADING THE BLIND.

12 Ap. 1832.

145.   BMC 16995   21 April 1832   Robert Seymour
A group of Tory peers surround a body that is representing the Reform Bill.
They dissect it, just as the Tories seek to mutilate the Bill in the House of Lords.
Lord Harrowby cuts off the left leg and shows it to Newcastle. Buckingham
cuts off the left arm. Wharncliffe cuts off the right arm. Cumberland cuts out
the heart. Wellington plunges a knife into the chest of the body. Lord Eldon
searches the victim's trouser pockets. Two bishops watch the mutilation.

INTERIOR OF THE TORY CHARNEL HOUSE.

146. BMC 17032 12 May 1832 Anonymous, but perhaps HB = John Doyle
A grey horse (Earl Grey), which is ridden by a terrified King, plunges into a
chasm. At the edge of the cliff is a warning: 'Beneath this Precipice lies the
fearful gulf of Revolution. Persons are warned not to approach the brink.' The
King seeks to save himself by grasping a branch (inscribed 'Lords') of the old
oak of the constitution, which has three branches (King, Lords and
Commons). The sun dazzles the horse with the 'wild fire of Reform'. The print
suggests that the King can save the country from revolution only by relying
upon the House of Lords which is threatening to defeat the Reform Bill once
more.

A FABLE FOR MINISTERS,

The Grey, its Rider — & the Wild Fire.

Published by Tho. McLean, 26 Haymarket, May 12th 1832.

WARNING

...

147.   BMC 17127   2 June 1832   Robert Seymour
William IV emulates King Canute by trying to stop the waves of the sea. The King acts under the influence of Wellington, Cumberland, Ellenborough and Lyndhurst. The waves reveal the heads of Grey and Brougham and are inscribed with the words 'Political Union'. On the horizon is the caption, 'The Ocean of Reform'.

THE OCEAN OF REFORM

POLITICAL UNION

HISTORY OF THE MODERN CANUTE.

148.	BMC 17136	June 1832	Robert Seymour
This is the frontispiece to a comic poem called *The Triumph of Reform*,
by W. T. Moncrieff. John Bull kicks two borough members, Wetherell
and Horace Twiss, from the doorway of the House of Commons,
while the Tory peers, Newcastle, Eldon, Cumberland and Wellington, are
threatened by a large broom (presumably wielded by Henry Brougham).

149. BMC 17143   c. June 1832   J. L. Marks

John Bull, with one foot on a block of stone labelled 'Reform', gazes at a cornucopia of coins, the 'land of promise', cheap bread and ale, 'no corn laws', etc. He is delighted at the prospect. This print illustrates one of the popular illusions about the social and economic consequences of the Reform Bill.

THE CHRONOLOGIST. N°.5

THE STEPING STONE; or John Bull peeping into Futurity !!!
Pub.d by J.L.Marks 91 Long Lane Smithfield.

150. BMC 17203   c. July 1832   J. L. Marks
This print illustrates the rapid disillusionment with the Reform Bill. A lean and ragged artisan, with a starving family, exclaims, 'In what better condition am I now that the *Reform Bill* has *past*!'.

THE MAN Wot pays the TAXES !!
London J.L.Marks Long Lane

FURTHER READING

For a detailed explanation of the prints and for attempts to set them in context see the relevant volumes in the British Museum's *Catalogue of Political and Personal Satires*, eds. F. G. Stephens and M. D. George.

For further information on political caricatures in this period, see M. Dorothy George, *English Political Caricature* (2 vols., Oxford, 1959); Herbert M. Atherton, *Political Prints in the Age of Hogarth* (Oxford, 1974); Charles Press, 'The Georgian Political Print and Democratic Institutions, *Comparative Studies in Society and History*, XIX (1977), pp. 216–38; M. D. George, 'America in English Satirical Prints', *William and Mary Quarterly*, 3rd series, X (1953), pp. 511–37; M. D. George, 'Pictorial Propaganda, 1793–1815: Gillray and Canning', *History*, XXXI (1946), pp. 9–25; John Brewer, 'The Faces of Lord Bute: A Visual Contribution to Anglo-American Political Ideology', *Perspectives in American History*, VI (1972), pp. 95–116; Rosemary Baker, 'Satirical Prints as a Source of English Social History', *Quarterly Journal of the Library of Congress* (Summer, 1982), pp. 132–45; H. T. Dickinson, 'A nice line in satire', *Times Higher Educational Supplement* (4 December 1981), pp. 12–13; John Wardroper, *The Caricatures of George Cruikshank* (London, 1977); and Draper Hill, *Mr. Gillray, The Caricaturist* (London, 1965).

For further reading on the arguments in favour of constitutional reform and in defence of the constitution in the period between 1760 and 1832, see John Cannon, *Parliamentary Reform 1640–1832* (Cambridge, 1973); E. and A. G. Porritt, *The Unreformed House of Commons* (2 vols., Cambridge, 1903–9); H. T. Dickinson, *Liberty and Property* (London, 1977); G. S. Veitch, *The Genesis of Parliamentary Reform* (London, 1913); Ian R. Christie, *Wilkes, Wyvill and Reform* (London, 1962); Edward Royle and James Walvin, *English Radicals and Reformers 1760–1848* (Brighton, 1982); E. C. Black, *The Association* (Cambridge Mass., 1963); Albert Goodwin, *The Friends of Liberty* (London, 1979); Malcolm I. Thomis and Peter Holt, *Threats of Revolution in Britain 1789–1848* (London, 1977); C. C. Bonwick, *English Radicals and the American Revolution* (Chapel Hill, 1977); A. S. Foord, *His Majesty's Opposition 1714–1830* (Oxford, 1964); Simon Maccoby, *English Radicalism, 1762–1832* (2 vols., London, 1955); R. R. Fennessy, *Burke, Paine and the Rights of Man* (The Hague, 1963); Austin Mitchell, *The Whigs in Opposition 1815–1830* (Oxford, 1967); John Stevenson, ed., *London in the Age of Reform* (Oxford, 1977); R. J. White, *Waterloo to Peterloo* (London, 1957); J. R. M. Butler, *The Passing of the Great Reform Act* (London, 1964); and Michael Brock, *The Great Reform Act* (London, 1973).